AF413765

CONQUERING CHAOS

STEVE MUSCATO

CONQUERING CHAOS

ALEXANDER THE GREAT'S WISDOM FOR LEADING IN DISRUPTIVE TIMES

Forbes | Books

Published by Forbes Books, Charleston, South Carolina.
An imprint of Advantage Media Group.

Forbes Books is a registered trademark, and the Forbes Books colophon is a trademark of Forbes Media, LLC.

Printed in the United States of America.

10 9 8 7 6 5 4 3 2 1

ISBN: 9798887507897 (Hardcover)
ISBN: 9798887507903 (eBook)
ISBN: 9798887507910 (Audiobook)

Library of Congress Control Number: 2026901164

Cover and layout design by David Taylor.

This custom publication is intended to provide accurate information and the opinions of the author in regard to the subject matter covered. It is sold with the understanding that the publisher, Forbes Books, is not engaged in rendering legal, financial, or professional services of any kind. If legal advice or other expert assistance is required, the reader is advised to seek the services of a competent professional.

Since 1917, Forbes has remained steadfast in its mission to serve as the defining voice of entrepreneurial capitalism. Forbes Books, launched in 2016 through a partnership with Advantage Media, furthers that aim by helping business and thought leaders bring their stories, passion, and knowledge to the forefront in custom books. Opinions expressed by Forbes Books authors are their own. To be considered for publication, please visit **books.Forbes.com**.

02-02-2026 7:41

CONTENTS

INTRODUCTION

It is the mark of an educated mind to be able to
entertain a thought without accepting it. –Aristotle

A framed list of leadership principles hangs on the wall above my computer screen, a constant, tangible reminder of timeless truths that have guided me through some of the most daunting professional challenges of my career. It's not some generic corporate vision statement, though. It's a distillation of insights drawn from an unlikely source: Alexander the Great. For decades, the Macedonian warrior king's audacious campaigns, intellectual curiosity, renowned charisma, and profound understanding of human nature have provided me with models of what to do and what not to do, inspiring and guiding me as a leader.

My journey to understanding leadership hasn't been linear, nor has it been confined to traditional business textbooks and education. It actually began with my lifelong passion for ancient history, especially the military and strategic minds that shaped civilizations. During my early career in the fast-paced world of energy trading, I noticed striking parallels between the strategic battles of antiquity and the fierce competition of modern markets. Money, in many ways, has become our new battlefield, where winners and losers emerge to real and meaningful effect. The "debris on the field"—the consequences of battle and its leadership decisions—is also just as real.

This realization sparked a deeper exploration: If ancient leaders faced such high stakes, what could their fundamental leadership principles teach us about navigating the modern corporate landscape? I discovered that the core drivers of both success and failure on ancient battlefields were remarkably similar to those of today's boardrooms and crisis command centers. The way good leaders motivated their people centuries ago, made decisions under pressure, and rallied their teams to overcome overwhelming odds holds profound lessons. Their leadership wasn't about brute force but a potent combination of knowledge, courage, and strength—a triad Alexander himself embodied. Alexander led from the front, earning the devotion of his soldiers, just as Maximus's unwavering courage and presence inspired fierce loyalty in Ridley Scott's *Gladiator*. This approach, I have learned, is not just for the battlefield. It is foundational for any leader seeking to navigate chaos with integrity.

This book is a deeply personal and practical guide to crisis leadership, blending Alexander's historical insights with my own real-world corporate challenges. My aim is to share the hard-won lessons from my experiences of leading through major crises and to offer both tactical strategies for decision-making under pressure and emotional insights into surviving the aftermath. It's an honest account that embraces failure, recovery, and the often-unspoken emotional toll that crisis takes on even the most prepared leaders.

The principles I've learned—often the hard way—have guided my executive career through events as diverse and devastating as the September 11 attacks in New York City and 2021's Winter Storm Uri in Texas. These experiences taught me that success in crisis is less about textbook answers and more about continuous learning, the ability to adapt, and a profound understanding of both the strategic landscape and the human element within your team. My journey has been one of constant evolution, moving from being a technically skilled but untested thirty-year-old leader during 9/11 to a more seasoned energy executive capable of navigating the existential threats of Winter Storm Uri twenty years later.

I wrote this book now because, throughout my career, I've seen too many leaders, often including myself, feel unprepared when true crisis hits. In my view, modern leadership training often focuses too heavily on success without adequately preparing leaders for failure and its difficult aftermath, including the emotional damage that leadership during disaster can inflict. Leaders need to understand that hardship is inevitable, but growth, learning, and resilience are what truly define leadership. This book aims to equip you with the strategic tools and the emotional strength to handle high-pressure situations with confidence and integrity.

The book walks the reader through the three distinct phases that create a complete cycle of leadership development:

- **Part I—Knowledge and Strength: The Foundations of Leadership.** Establishing the necessary groundwork for effective crisis leadership means following Alexander the Great's example of combining intellectual preparation and practical strength. For modern leaders, this means combining preparation, education, and team building to build a firm, integrated foundation.

- **Part II—Into the Fire: Confronting Crisis.** How do great leaders make decisions in the midst of active crisis? Under extreme pressure and with incomplete information, leaders in the midst of crisis management face a trial by fire where theories are tested against harsh realities. At the Battle of Gaugamela in 331 BCE, Alexander executed a daring tactical maneuver to defeat the Persian army, which vastly outnumbered his forces, by studying the terrain and anticipating enemy movements.

- **Part III—The Indus Principle: Into New Territories.** The aftermath of crisis can be transformation when hard-won wisdom becomes the foundation for future leadership. Focusing on healing, growth, and legacy building in the wake of unforeseen events ensures that leadership and teams do not merely return to normal but evolve into new strength. At the Battle of the Hydaspes in 326 BCE, Alexander commanded a diverse army of Macedonians, Persians, and Indian allies that was very different from the all-European army he commanded when he started the invasion of the Persian Empire.

Just as Alexander's campaigns transformed him from prince to king to legend, your leadership journey can transform you too … *if* you have the courage to take lessons from both victory and defeat. By learning from ancient examples and my own very modern experiences, you will come away from this book better equipped to lead with confidence and wisdom while handling the unknown, whether it be new technology, staff turnover, or a major crisis.

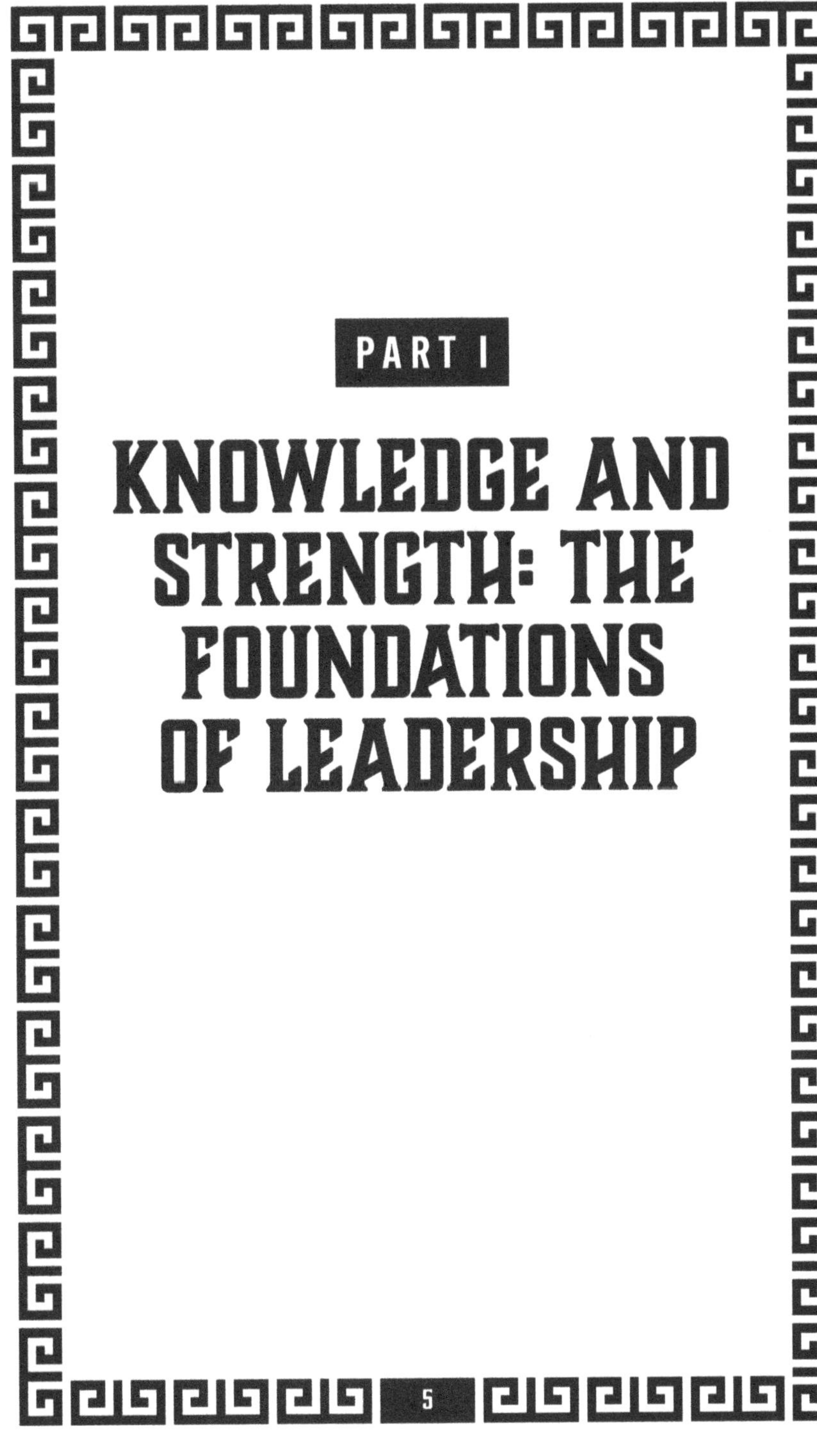

PART I
KNOWLEDGE AND STRENGTH: THE FOUNDATIONS OF LEADERSHIP

THE ANCIENT AND THE MODERN

There is nothing impossible to him who
will try. –Alexander the Great

The phone rang, jolting me awake at half-past one in the morning. It was February of 2021. The voice on the other end was urgent, bordering on panicked. "Steve, I don't know who you have to call, but if we don't shed more load, we're gonna lose the grid in four minutes."

Winter Storm Uri had hit Texas with a ferocity that far surpassed any forecast. At the time, I was the chief commercial officer at Vistra Corporation, the largest competitive power generator in the US, providing essential power resources across Texas and nationwide. Like every power company, we always kept an eye on the weather, but the numbers our meteorologists had given us a week prior, indicating a "historic storm," had underestimated its intensity. We had assumed linear load growth—that electricity consumption would increase proportionally with temperature drops. Instead, it went exponential, something we had never seen before in our modern records. The demand for power was so immense that it was pulling the frequency of the entire Texas grid down, triggering power plants to trip offline to protect themselves. We were minutes away from a total black start—having to restore electric power stations to operation without being able to rely on the external network—a weeks-long process that would have been an unprecedented catastrophe. The weight of responsibility in that moment was immense. Millions of Texans depended on our decisions.

In those chaotic moments as we scrambled to prevent total collapse, I wasn't consciously thinking, *What would Alexander the Great do?* However, the core leadership lessons that had been ingrained in me throughout my career—many of them inspired by Alexander's philosophy—guided my every move. This unforeseen crisis forced us to throw out our playbook and think differently. We had to think carefully, think quickly, and use logic, anchoring ourselves on a clear hierarchy of principles: Safety had to come first, always. But otherwise, we were without a map.

My connection to Alexander the Great began not in this crisis but during the quiet moments parents treasure, reading to my daughter at bedtime about his conquests. We'd discuss the good, and importantly, the "less good," aspects of historical figures. I love sharing my passion for history, and I had a great role model for discussing big ideas in my own father, who often challenged me with deep concepts as a kid. Alexander was a military genius, his tactics studied to this day, but his life wasn't without problematic elements. I think it's important to acknowledge this without judging him too harshly through a modern lens. For instance, his ruthless approach to succession and his decisions to eliminate companions suspected of disloyalty would be abhorrent today. Yet from these "shadow sides" of Alexander, we can extract powerful lessons on what *not* to do, just as we learn about what we *should* do from his strengths.

What initially drew me to Alexander, and what remains profoundly relevant for modern leaders, were his education and approach to knowledge. Tutored by none other than Aristotle, Alexander learned critical and logical thinking in a way that was unique for his time. While others might have relied solely on religious omens or superstition, Alexander was taught that the universe can be understood through reason. This philosophical foundation, emphasizing observation and the power of the human brain, was a precursor to the scientific method.

This approach, plus his intellectual curiosity, allowed Alexander to see beyond conventional wisdom. Aristotle, for example, taught Alexander that the Persians were barbarians and not equals of the Greeks. Yet, when Alexander conquered Babylon and observed the sophisticated achievements of Persian culture, he concluded that people who could create such wonders couldn't be barbaric. He recognized the value in their culture and later even embraced Persian customs, integrating them into his empire.

Alexander's multiculturalism and openness to different perspectives are lessons I've carried throughout my career, actively seeking out diverse viewpoints from colleagues from around the world to gain a more holistic understanding of problems and solutions. When an issue occurs, I can tap into the unique perspectives my colleagues willingly and fearlessly provide, thanks to the trust I try to cultivate in my relationships. These connections are invaluable. For example, in the early stages of the COVID-19 global pandemic, I was able to ask a colleague in China what was happening on the ground. His input was critical to my ability to get ahead of the news cycle and prepare our company before others could begin. In another moment, I was able to ask a colleague of mine from Russia about the probability of Russia invading Ukraine during the buildup to that crisis. His insights were pivotal in preparing my company for the eventual outcome.

The Modern Leadership Crisis

In today's volatile world, many leaders, sometimes including me, feel profoundly unprepared when a real crisis hits. The sheer speed, scale, and complexity of modern disruptions—whether natural disasters, market disruptions, or unforeseen global pandemics—can feel overwhelming. When times are good, we tend to live with what cognitive scientists call an *optimism bias*: the belief that those good times will last indefinitely. The economic boom of the 1990s, for instance, fostered a sense that major disruptions were a thing of the past. Then 9/11 happened, and the unthinkable became reality.

What's often missing from modern leadership training is not just cultivating the ability to respond to crisis but preparing for failure and providing guidance for the aftermath. We focus on success and rarely acknowledge the unspoken emotional damage and personal toll of high-stakes decision-making. This book addresses these gaps head-on, aiming to normalize the fact that leadership in crisis is rarely perfect but always transformative.

Years before Winter Storm Uri, I was a thirty-year-old vice president at TXU (currently Vistra Corporation) in Dallas, Texas, when 9/11 happened—a moment of crisis I was vastly unprepared to lead through. I was in charge of energy trading for the Northeast region, buying and selling power and natural gas throughout the

Northeast in ways similar to how Wall Street traders buy and sell stocks. Cantor Fitzgerald, which then occupied the 101st to 105th floors of One World Trade Center, was my company's broker. My team had relationships with Cantor Fitzgerald's employees and direct phone connections to their offices as the attack unfolded. It was horrifying to experience.

At that time in my life, I was technically skilled as an engineer, but my leadership was largely untested for a crisis of that magnitude. There was no playbook to consult, and I learned painful lessons about accepting impossible assignments and failing to speak truth to power.

At thirty, filled with youthful confidence, I had taken on a task others deemed impossible, believing my team and I were "that good." The task was to make money for the company by speculatively trading gas and power in a region of the country where we had limited experience, a small regulatory presence, and at least in those days, no power plants. In the immediate aftermath of 9/11, as we were working to hit our financial objectives, my team was also trying to locate the last voice recordings left by their friends at Cantor Fitzgerald to send to their families. I was too naive and green to recognize that my team's heads were not in the game. I had yet to learn when to prioritize people and when to de-risk. I kept driving my team forward, pushing them too hard, much like Alexander underestimated the emotional and physical limits of his troops at the Hyphasis River (now called the Beas River) in India.

In 326 BCE, the mutiny on the banks of the Hyphasis marked a pivotal historical turning point in Alexander the Great's campaigns, revealing an unbridgeable gap between his ambition and his army's exhaustion. Through his brilliant leadership, Alexander had conquered territory spanning from Greece through Persia and India, essentially the known world at the time. And he had a vision to push even deeper into the Indian subcontinent. His goal was to conquer the rich and powerful kingdoms beyond the Ganges River.

At the Hyphasis, however, Alexander's troops, weary from nearly a decade of continuous warfare, reached their breaking point. The monsoon rains, dense jungles, foreign diseases, and fierce resistance from Indian kingdoms took a significant toll on morale. (Not to mention that the elephants the Persians used in battle terrified the horses!) The men longed for home and rest.

The troops staged a strike, refusing to march further east. Coenus, one of Alexander's trusted generals, spoke on their behalf, urging Alexander to abandon his plans. He told Alexander that the soldiers' spirits were broken and their bodies spent. Coenus, a brilliant military leader in his own right, emphasized that a wise leader knew when to stop and consolidate rather than stretch resources and morale to the breaking point. Despite Alexander's initial fury and disappointment, Coenus's speech clearly resonated. Alexander was forced to concede and retreat.

For the first time in his career, Alexander the Great, who had conquered the mighty Persian Empire and never known defeat, faced resistance not from his enemies but from within his own ranks. Though he withdrew with dignity, erecting twelve massive altars to mark the eastern boundary of his empire and to commemorate his gods and achievements, the Hyphasis Mutiny exposed the limits of imperial ambition in the face of human endurance.

The mutiny at the Hyphasis River underscored a fundamental truth: Even the greatest military commander cannot rule without the will of their people. It was a dramatic moment in history that forced Alexander to face the reality that conquest has limits—not just geographic but *human.*

That human lesson that Alexander painfully learned was one I likewise learned in the chaos and collective agony of 9/11. As I mentioned previously, one of the energy brokers we used to facilitate business at that time was Cantor Fitzgerald, which had offices on floors 101 to 105 of One World Trade Center, above the point of impact by the first plane. We had developed close relationships with the Cantor Fitzgerald team throughout the years, and my team was distraught after hearing that our colleagues had to go up to the roof of the building to avoid the flames below. You could hear the shock in the room as the first tower fell. We knew what it meant for the people on the roof.

My team did not strike in the classical sense, but their understandable emotional reactions to the horrifying events in which we'd lost our colleagues and friends created resistance that meant we couldn't achieve our objectives. I didn't recognize this, nor did I realize I needed to step back, de-risk the company's financial exposure, and prioritize the human side of the equation, allowing my team to heal. De-risking the company's position would mean closing out any open energy positions to eliminate the financial exposure to moving prices, then reassessing as both the situation and people's anxiety calmed. Instead, we maintained existing energy positions and continued to look for new opportunities at a time when we did not have the strength to support the effort. This failure became one of my most transformative leadership lessons. It still causes me pain to this day, but I try to see the gift in what that horrible time taught me.

In the *Harvard Business Review,* professor of organizational behavior Gianpiero Petriglieri reflects on the value of leaders who can "hold," or contain and interpret, the events and experiences of crisis:[1]

> People never forget how managers treated them when they were facing loss. And we will remember how our institutions, managers, and peers, held us through this crisis—or failed to. We also see the consequences of past failures of holding, in those institutions struggling to mobilize an already depleted pool of resources. It is tempting to resort to command and control in a crisis, but it is leaders who hold instead that help us work through it. And it is to those leaders, I believe, that we'll turn to when time comes to articulate a vision for the future.

The personal toll of crisis, particularly the emotional damage, is something leadership books rarely discuss. When Winter Storm Uri descended upon Texas, it was unlike anything seen in modern times, quickly becoming a defining, almost career-destroying challenge for me and my company. I literally remember coming home and saying to my wife, "Well, it's been a good run." The storm hit with far more intensity than projected, and things quickly began to fall apart.

The demand for power as the storm worsened and temperatures plummeted created a load so immense it began to pull down the frequency of the grid, causing power plants to trip offline to protect themselves. This created a cascading series of outages. The Electric

---

1   Gianpiero Petriglieri, "The Psychology Behind Effective Crisis Leadership," *Harvard Business Review,* April 22, 2020, https://hbr.org/2020/04/the-psychology-behind-effective-crisis-leadership.

Reliability Council of Texas (ERCOT), the organization responsible for balancing the operations of the electrical system, made the critical decision to aggressively shed load, leading to chaotic, rather than controlled, rolling outages. This desperate measure prevented total collapse. It also created, essentially, a state of anarchy: ERCOT didn't know what critical infrastructure it was shutting off. We had to coordinate rapidly to ensure power plants didn't lose critical water supply or natural gas connections. It was an adrenaline-filled, horrifically stressful situation.

By the next evening, the situation had worsened. Because of gas production freezing and the strong use of natural gas by power plants, the gas system began to show signs of physical stress. Gas pressures were critically low, gas prices were skyrocketing, and all our initial assumptions turned out to be wrong. We had to throw out the operating principles we'd relied on for twenty years. I remember pulling my team into a huddle and making a stark directive: "I don't care if the gas is $400, you have to buy it. We have to buy all the gas that's out there. Forget about the price. Stop looking at the price. Just buy it." It was simply what needed to be done.

This crisis demanded unprecedented solutions and extensive coordination with external partners, including state and federal governments. We had fuel oil trucks rolling behind snowplows, worked with government officials to instruct liquefied natural gas exporters to stop exporting and thus keep gas in Texas, and negotiated with the Occupational Safety and Health Administration for hours exceptions for essential workers. To maintain power output, decisions were made to allow power plants to temporarily exceed normal emission limits. It was about saving the population from freezing. We had to map the entire chain, from power plants needing gas to pipelines needing electricity, making real-time, split-second decisions to save the system.

The financial toll of the storm was immense. Vistra lost an astounding $2 billion—yes, "billion" with a *B*—in a single week. But that was only part of what made the storm so devastating. Cities across the state, such as San Antonio, suffered massive losses, with some even going bankrupt because of the exorbitant costs. Some natural gas utilities also took huge hits, having to borrow money and spread the financial burden to their customers over decades.

For my team, the immediate aftermath was one of shame, exhaustion, and frustration. We were hit from all sides, with reliability and safety investigations from the state and accountability demands from Vistra's board about the $2 billion loss. It certainly felt like the end of our careers. We were learning a hard, fast lesson: The crisis itself may not be the hardest part. The aftermath can be even harder.

The investigations were long but necessary. It was a period of intense grief, stress, and anxiety. We had gotten through the crisis itself, though, and so we struggled to understand why we still felt so bad. I brought in a counselor to support our team after the grueling experience. The counselor recognized signs of intense stress and exhaustion in us, similar to what he had seen from people in other high-stress situations. We resisted the diagnosis at first, since we did not want to compare our situation to the far greater traumas that are out there. The counselor said that regardless, we still carried the signs of stress and exhaustion. This resonated deeply and helped us acknowledge our experience. Millions had relied on us to prevent catastrophic failure, and despite our relentless efforts, things didn't always go as planned. We learned to accept that our feelings were valid, a natural response to the situation, and that they did not diminish our strength as a team or organization. That realization was the first step toward moving forward with clarity and resilience.

The Journey Ahead

Across its three sections, this book leads the reader through elemental experiences of leadership that reflect both Alexander's journey and my own.

PREPARATION

This phase of a leader's experience involves building knowledge and strength before crisis hits. It means not just studying historical data but also daring to think about the possibility of shifts that go far beyond typical "extreme" predictions. For example, what if natural gas prices skyrocketed not just to twenty dollars per unit, something a typical disaster plan might consider, but to hundreds? Like many companies, the companies I worked for had risk models that mapped out disaster and recovery scenarios. But what my companies and I encountered turned out to be far from what anyone predicted. The world's complexity demands that we think far beyond where we imagine the limits to lie, and simultaneously, that we understand that there are differences of opinion regarding what's likely to be true in terms of risks present and future. This comes up especially with politically charged topics such as climate change and preparing for worst-case scenarios. Effective preparation takes this into account. It also involves proactive communication strategies: assessing whom to tell and what to tell them if we are to avoid being perceived as a Chicken Little, while still ensuring that critical information reaches the right stakeholders, from CEOs to state governors.

CONFRONTATION

In this phase, everything is at stake, and we must lead through the fire. Confrontations hinge on adaptability and making decisions without complete information. We rely on our preparation and remember the core principles we've crafted, even when the financial stakes are astronomical. Navigating confrontation is also about being aware of your team's stress, stepping back when needed, and being present on the ground with your people, not solely at the helm of the battleship. I manage so differently now than I did during 9/11. During Winter Storm Uri, my team and I worked twenty-hour days, sleeping for only four hours a night in a nearby hotel—all during the COVID-19 pandemic, before vaccines were widely available. I was not merely directing my team; I was in the trenches with them. In those high-pressure moments, the preparation of years spent building mutual trust and loyalty became critical.

AFTERMATH AND BEYOND

Crises end, but not without cost and consequences. As I learned from Winter Storm Uri, a crisis is not over when the immediate danger is over, because that is when the investigations and emotional reckoning begin. I have always striven to be ethical, and even though I understood it was necessary, putting my decisions and ethics under the microscope was painful. I wasn't well prepared to deal with the shame, exhaustion, and intense scrutiny. I learned to distinguish between responsibility and blame, to embrace transparency, and to provide and seek support for myself and my team. Moments of external validation, such as when a board member told me "It wasn't your fault" after Winter Storm Uri, also helped me integrate the experience of crisis into my leadership identity. When we understand that even failures contribute to growth, we find emotional recovery, resilience, and new ways to prepare for the next challenge. Leadership education is a continuing conversation, not just a formal learning process, and through this conversation, diverse experiences and perspectives shape a more holistic view of problems and solutions. The foundations of future leadership have their roots in hard-won wisdom.

The Alexander Promise

I didn't write this book because I got everything right. I wrote it because Alexander's example and my own experience show that a blend of practical leadership strategies, techniques for emotional resilience in crisis, proven team-building approaches that withstand intense pressure, and essential healing practices for after the battle ends can be transformative. Just as Alexander's campaigns elevated him from a king to a legend, I believe your leadership journey can elevate you, equipping you with the wisdom and courage to navigate your own unique challenges with confidence and integrity.

Thinking through Alexander's examples in combination with present-day experiences can help you develop the critical thinking skills to anticipate threats, the boldness to take calculated risks that intimidate adversaries, and a profound understanding of your team's human needs that ensures loyalty and resilience, not mutiny. We will explore how preparing for the unexpected means looking beyond historical data to understand how cascades of second- and third-order effects can turn seemingly distant global events into deeply personal crises for your organization and its people.

Looking Ahead

The purpose of this book is to ensure that leaders are prepared not just for managing crises but also for navigating the personal and professional aftermath.

In the next chapter, we will explore the education of a leader, examining how proper training and mentorship prepare leaders for crisis moments, much as Aristotle prepared Alexander long before he ever led an army into battle. We'll explore the essential knowledge and guidance that are needed long before facing defining challenges and consider how both formal education and life experiences are the foundation for everything that follows, shaping a leader's ability to make decisions under pressure and build the knowledge and strength necessary to confront the unknown.

THE EDUCATION OF A LEADER

Without knowledge, skill cannot be focused. Without skill, strength cannot be brought to bear, and without strength, knowledge may not be applied. –Alexander the Great

For any leader facing the overwhelming chaos of a crisis, the path forward isn't always clear. There's no perfect playbook, no guaranteed success. But what can truly make the difference, as I've learned repeatedly throughout my career, is that obtaining the right education and mentorship long before any storm hits is absolutely foundational to navigating these defining moments. This isn't just about formal degrees or certifications. Instead, I am talking about a deeper, more personal, and mettle-tested development that shapes how you think, how you connect with people, and how you act when everything is on the line.

Alexander's Unique Curriculum

Alexander the Great's education was, without a doubt, one of the most remarkable we know of in his time: a young prince tutored by Aristotle himself. I try to imagine what that experience must have been like. What did Alexander learn that set him apart from other rulers, such as the Persian kings, who in Aristotle's view were "corrupt" and "barbarian"?

Aristotle's teaching was primarily focused on critical thinking and logical reasoning. Philosophers the world over still revere his approach. Greek philosophy, which laid the groundwork for the scientific method, emphasized that the universe could be understood through human reason and observation. Alexander wasn't taught to passively await answers from oracles or advisors but to actively seek and build his own understanding. This was the difference that made him a once-in-a-millennium ruler.

One manifestation of classical Greek philosophy's logical approach is what's often referred to as the Socratic method, a system of breaking down problems by asking questions rather than making assumptions. Alexander learned to analyze situations through asking questions and making observations. Long practice with this mode of collecting evidence and asking questions about it gave him a pathway to apply the theoretical knowledge he'd gleaned from studying philosophy, politics, ethics, and the natural sciences. He combined this with intense practical military training, particularly under his father, Philip II, and General Parmenion. These great leaders taught him not just to push enemies off the field but to encircle and decisively annihilate them. Alexander's military training therefore provided yet another component which, combined with logic, observation, and questioning, contributed to his ability to make incredibly fast and effective decisions on the battlefield that led to unprecedented victories.

Alexander's capacity for keen observation enabled him to think outside the box in multiple ways. In a famous example from his early life, he was tasked with taming Bucephalus, a supposedly untamable horse. When Alexander realized what others had not—that the horse was simply afraid of his own shadow—he calmly approached, turned Bucephalus's head so he could no longer see it, and was able to tame him. This moment demonstrated Alexander's unique problem-solving ability and courage, impressing his father and creating a bond between the prince and that special steed.

It is a testament to Alexander's own perceptive genius that his education allowed him to see even beyond what Aristotle had taught him. While Aristotle's worldview did not tend to embrace other cultures, Alexander recognized their value through his own observations, ultimately embracing a multicultural approach that even led him to incorporate Persian customs and leadership into his own practices. This capacity for cultural integration and adapting to different perspectives became a hallmark of Alexander's vision as he matured.

My Own Leadership Education: From Engineering to Empathy

Much like Alexander's, my personal leadership education was a blend of formal training and crucial, at times painful, real-world "battlefield" experiences. My formal background is in engineering. This discipline taught me how to think, how to break down complex problems into manageable pieces, and how to solve problems logically and within defined parameters. It's a very analytical, science-based approach that resonates deeply with the Greek principles of observation and reason. It's the reason why the Socratic method—asking questions to understand and break down problems, rather than simply dictating solutions—became a core part of my leadership style.

However, my engineering mindset also presented a hurdle. In the precise, data-driven world of engineering, you strive to collect all the facts before acting. In trading, by contrast, you have to make quick decisions with incomplete information—a theme that comes up throughout this book. As a result, when I transitioned from engineering to trading, I quickly encountered the weakness of "analysis paralysis." I had to force myself to adapt and learn to combine the "what I know" of facts and logical analysis with the "what I believe" of experience and intuition, based on my experience and understanding of human behavior, in order to make actionable decisions without hesitation. This was a career necessity: I wouldn't have succeeded without making that leap. This skill became crucial during crises such as Winter Storm Uri, when the playbook had to be rewritten on the fly, requiring immediate but reasoned decisions under immense pressure.

Beyond my formal education, two key experiences from my early career profoundly shaped my leadership approach. The first of these were dinner table debates with my dad. My father, a union electrician, would spark discussions at the dinner table that fostered original thought and a global perspective. This taught me that complex problems often have multiple sides and perspectives; not everything is black and white. I learned the importance of listening, articulating my own points, and critically, how to compromise and live in ambiguity to achieve collective goals. These debates also helped me understand the cascading "downhill effects" of global events on local situations, a crucial insight for any leader. I had to think beyond our dinner table and out into the world.

The other experience was adopting the practice of learning from and involving people at all levels, something I picked up as a twenty-year-old intern at General Motors. In that role, I needed union electricians to complete tasks. Some of these guys were double or even triple my age, with lots of experience, and as they say, these men didn't suffer fools gladly. My father's advice was invaluable: "Listen to people in the trenches, and seek advice from them to solve problems." Instead of a top-down approach of giving orders, I learned to engage with the electricians, listen to their concerns—sometimes over donuts and coffee—and involve them in problem-solving and even design processes. Doing this taught me that technical expertise isn't enough. Leadership requires understanding people, their motivations, and the hidden cultures behind how things truly get done. It showed me that true leadership is about the ability to motivate people regardless of direct reporting lines, not about authority. This learning process also cultivated my "management by walking around" approach, something that's kept me connected to the front lines throughout my career and was especially important during my trading years.

My early experiences revealed a significant gap between a theoretical business education and the messy reality of real-world management. Business school might teach you models and theories, but it can't teach you how to apply them when human behavior introduces ambiguity or when you face unprecedented situations. A 2016 *Harvard Business Review* analysis reflected that CEOs with MBAs do not perform better than those without; in other words, the degree a

CEO has earned is not necessarily critical to their success.[2] To make the best possible decisions in the face of uncertainty takes a combination of foundational knowledge, critical thinking, and a deep understanding of the human element.

Leading through crisis, therefore, isn't just about formal education, and it isn't just about tactical execution either. It's a profound test of one's entire education, formal and informal. How well have you learned to think, to adapt, and to understand the human equation in a crisis? Can you turn every challenge into a lesson that refines your leadership skills?

The Unprepared Leader

My own leadership education began long before I fully understood its necessity. At age thirty, during the 9/11 attacks, I found myself in a senior leadership role. I was technically skilled, but my leadership was fundamentally untested. It was a jarring awakening. I was a vice president, and my immediate superiors, including the company president, effectively collapsed under the pressure, both physically and emotionally. One or two were gently escorted out of the building, crying. There was a desperate search for leadership.

In that moment, I realized that nothing whatsoever in my educational background had prepared me for the crisis. It was not merely the initial shock, the hesitation as the whole world was blindsided. It was also that there was no one leading *me*. The senior vice president called a meeting but essentially told us we were on our own. There was going to be no guidance from above. No one was going to tell

---

2   Daniel McGinn, "Resisting the Lure of Short-Termism," *Harvard Business Review*, November 2016, https://hbr.org/2016/11/the-best-performing-ceos-in-the-world.

me the right thing to do, if there even was a right thing to do. It was a crisis management scenario brand-new to all of us.

I, too, felt that initial paralysis, asking myself, "What do I do now?" Like the whole world, I was numb. Like many crises, it was unimaginable and unforeseen. There was no emergency manual, no standard operating procedures for something of this magnitude. When no senior leadership stepped up with guidance, I had to fill that void, and I was unprepared for the scale of it.

I was thrust into this leadership role prematurely. Driven by fear of losing my job, especially with a new house and a baby, I accepted what I can now see in hindsight was an impossible assignment, a job others were turning down. I believed I had to push through the panic and throw emotion aside to get the job done. This was precisely my misstep: I failed to recognize or address the profound emotional toll the crisis was taking on my team.

In the aftermath of the attacks, my team members were processing the last words our colleagues and friends at Cantor Fitzgerald had left on voicemail, wanting to provide these to their grieving families. As I mentioned in chapter 1, this was my Hyphasis moment. Instead of pressing pause on the financial objectives that were our everyday goals and allowing my team to process, I was pushing them to do both, effectively marching them to a point where, like Alexander's army at the river, they didn't want to go any further. In my immaturity, I was leading the team in such a way that they didn't want to follow me. I recognized this after I gave them an assignment, but then found that, rather than working on it, the team was focusing on collecting the last phone recordings from the brokers at Cantor Fitzgerald so they could send those recordings to the brokers' loved ones. My team needed to know that, amid the chaos, they could do something to help others.

This painful failure became one of my most transformative leadership lessons.

Like most leaders, I began my career unprepared for a true crisis. Modern leadership training often focuses on success without adequately preparing for failure or providing guidance for navigating its emotional aftermath. This creates leaders who are expected to make high-stakes decisions but who are ill-equipped for the consequences or personal toll of that decision-making. The cost of learning leadership lessons in real time during high-stakes situations can be immense, both financially and in terms of human impact.

Building Your Leadership Foundation

Great leaders never stop learning. For me, learning has come not only through books or classrooms but through conversations with people whose different backgrounds and opinions have given me a more holistic understanding of problems and potential solutions. As a leader, I have always been curious about the next generations and what motivates them, as well as about global events. I am an avid consumer of information and am always keen to gain insights from the real world. When my company sent me for a two-week class at Columbia Business School, it served as a valuable refresher that allowed me to indulge my passion for learning and think more deeply about leadership. I also listen to The Great Courses Plus on my phone, which includes lectures on many topics from many different universities. One of my favorites among these offerings is a thirty-six-part series called *Alexander the Great and the Macedonian Empire*. I enjoyed this course as I prepared to write this book and was excited to learn a few things I did not already know despite being a passionate student of Alexander's history!

My commitment to learning and openness has strengthened the foundations of my leadership. For example, after years of navigating high-stakes environments, I've developed an expert intuition that allows me to make fast, effective decisions without requiring a full deck of data, lengthy reports, or endless presentations. This kind of decision-making isn't guesswork. It's not just a "hunch" or a gut feeling. In his seminal book *Thinking, Fast and Slow*, psychologist Daniel Kahneman warns that intuition alone can be misleading or unreliable, countering that it must be grounded in experience and ongoing learning.[3] The most effective decision-making is the product of accumulated experience, thousands of decisions made in real time and often under pressure, and lessons learned from both wins and failures.

What once took hours or days for me to analyze and think through now often takes only minutes. After years of immersion in complex systems and people dynamics, I've learned to trust my ability to identify the signals, patterns, and responses that emerge. As a leader, this means I can quickly and confidently evaluate ambiguous or high-pressure situations, even if all the variables aren't yet visible. The capacity to make swift, accurate judgments despite uncertainty is one of the most valuable leadership tools I've acquired. I know I am a far different leader now than I was at thirty. I had intuition at thirty—all of us have intuition at every age, of course. But my intuition today has been tested, tempered in the fire of crisis, and is informed by more experience.

---

3   Daniel Kahneman, *Thinking, Fast and Slow* (Farrar, Straus and Giroux, 2011).

Thus, true leadership education is a continuous, multifaceted journey, blending formal knowledge with the invaluable, often messy lessons of real-world experience. You learn leadership much as a chef learns to cook. You start with the formal education of recipes and instructors, but *real* mastery comes from countless hours in the kitchen, adapting to unexpected ingredients, sampling new dishes and spices, learning what each can bring to your dishes, and paying attention to the evolving tastes of your diners and their special, diverse needs.

The path forward isn't always clear for any leader facing the overwhelming chaos of a crisis. But developing this deeper approach can shape how you think, how you connect with people, and how you act when everything is on the line. It cannot be a superficial approach. It has to run deep, all the way to the bedrock of who you are.

Part of this lies in looking to see what information may already be out there. Consider the story of Xenophon's account of the Persian Empire, which influenced Alexander's journey. Cyrus the Younger had hired Xenophon and his ten thousand Greek mercenaries to overthrow his brother Artaxerxes, the Persian king. Cyrus failed to oust his brother, but in the wake of that defeat, the Greeks were able to fight their way back to Greece, through hostile Persian territory, by taking advantage of what they'd learned about the weaknesses of the Persian military and surrounding territories. That historical account helped me understand that it is possible to overcome even superpowers by having the humility to gather information from others who may have already faced the challenge you are attempting. There is no point in reinventing the wheel if there is already a body of work out there on the problem.

The Balance Between Confidence and Humility in Leadership Education

Leadership demands a delicate equilibrium of confidence and humility. History offers us powerful examples of this, few more striking than the life of Alexander the Great. While widely celebrated and admired as a military prodigy and strategic mastermind, Alexander's extraordinary self-confidence could veer into dangerous territory. His unwavering self-reliance allowed him to boldly confront formidable enemies, often succeeding where others would have hesitated. His ability to trust his instincts and push boundaries was in many ways what made him legendary. But there was a shadow side to that confidence, an arrogance that, over time, alienated many of his most senior commanders and advisors. Some of his officers felt marginalized or even disregarded, especially when Alexander began to believe that only he possessed the insight or clarity to make crucial decisions. This was on display when Alexander adopted Persian customs such as *proskynesis* (prostration), alienating some of his senior commanders, including Cleitus the Black. At a banquet in 328 BCE, Alexander's claim of divine insight provoked Cleitus, who felt marginalized and disrespected. The argument escalated and Alexander, enraged, killed Cleitus, showing that Alexander's confidence not only strained some loyal relationships but fatally ended them.

When Alexander relied too heavily on himself and discounted the wisdom and perspectives of others, it ultimately created distance between Alexander and those around him. In many ways, Alexander's savant-like brilliance shielded him from the fallout that would have doomed a lesser leader. Had a leader without Alexander's genius adopted the same postures or made the same demands, the results likely would have been catastrophic—fragmented teams, poor morale, or outright mutiny. Alexander's example, therefore, serves as a cautionary one. Confidence is essential to leadership, particularly for decisive action under pressure, but it must be balanced with humility or it may become isolating, even corrosive.

We see this today. The world is full of stories of CEOs, especially recent ones, known for bad behavior such as bullying. In some cases, a CEO's brilliance or status may convince others to tolerate what really isn't—or shouldn't be—tolerable. Great leaders, alternatively, bring people along with them as they make decisions. This requires listening, acknowledging one's limitations, and being open to input and correction.

My own leadership journey has been shaped by learning this balance the hard way. Early in my career, especially in the tumultuous period following 9/11, I made critical errors in judgment that stemmed from a lack of emotional maturity. At the time, I was young, relatively inexperienced, and if I'm honest, operating from a place of fear. In my case, fear masked itself as drive, which in turn led me to push my team far too hard. I expected them to perform at maximum capacity without fully acknowledging or addressing the psychological and emotional strain they were under following the 9/11 attacks that had hit us all so close to home. My team members were carrying immense burdens—grief, trauma, anxiety—and yet I pressed forward as if productivity alone would be our salvation.

That experience was humbling and deeply painful. It forced me to confront the extremes of what leadership can demand of people, especially in times of crisis. I learned that every team has a breaking point and that it's the leader's responsibility to understand where that threshold lies. Alexander had to learn that lesson as well when his team refused to go any further at the Hyphasis River in 326 BCE. His exhausted army, after years of grueling campaigns, refused to march further into India. Leadership isn't about extracting every last ounce of effort from people. It's about caring for them well enough that they can sustain their energy, their trust, and their loyalty through difficulty. 9/11 changed how I lead forever because it humbled me.

Humility, I've come to understand, is not weakness. It's the strength to recognize when you're wrong, when someone else has a better idea, and when the team needs something different from what you originally planned. Having humility means letting go of pride of authorship—that attachment to your own way of doing things—and embracing solid input from anywhere it originates. Some of the best ideas I've implemented have come from people on the front lines, not executives in boardrooms. Early in the COVID-19 pandemic, we had an energy analytics director who had family in China explaining to us, in advance of the news cycle, the panic that was gripping the city of Wuhan. Thanks to his consistent reports, we were better prepared for the coming situation and were able to more effectively protect our people and firm by educating senior leaders of the conditions on the ground in Wuhan and extrapolating that to places around the world.

Today, I actively look for humility in others. In interviews, one of my go-to questions is, "Tell me about your biggest failure and what you learned from it." That question reveals a lot. People who can reflect openly and honestly on their failures usually demonstrate the kind of growth mindset I want on my team. They're not afraid to own their missteps, learn from them, and evolve. And that, ultimately, is what humility in leadership is all about: not putting yourself down, but being grounded enough to keep learning, keep listening, and keep growing—and to help others do the same.

Preparing the Next Generation

A critical aspect of leadership is preparing future generations. I approach mentoring my team members by actively investing in them as people. I look for individuals with integrity, humility, and ambition, then give them "stretch assignments," trusting in their ability to learn and grow from the challenge. Many of my direct reports have evolved alongside me over two decades, reaching their own significant career milestones en route, which brings me great satisfaction. Leadership is not about the leader, but what they can do to develop those who will carry the company forward.

The importance of preparing teams for crisis before it arrives cannot be overstated. My transformative 9/11 experience taught me the painful lesson of pushing a team past its limits. Having learned this, I deliberately gave my team members permission to take breaks as needed during Winter Storm Uri. I knew that people would respond differently to stress, and a leader must be both aware of this and calm about the inevitability that it will occur. I can remember one worker whose family was without power, with a pregnant wife and young child at home. I realized his mind could not possibly be on our crisis, only on the one unfolding in his home. I urged him to go spend a couple of hours ensuring his family was safe and then to come back. There were no repercussions, no shame, no pressure to remain.

We'll explore this more in the next chapter, but over years of shared experience, my team had already internalized logical thinking, loyalty, and the motivation to fight both for each other and, when necessary, *with* each other. This established loyalty and mutual trust meant that when Winter Storm Uri hit, our collective responses were ingrained like muscle memory, allowing us to adapt quickly when the existing playbook became useless, and we had to reinvent it on the fly.

When I share Alexander's lessons, whether with my daughter or my team, I discuss his entire legacy, both the good parts and the less good. For instance, Alexander's tactical brilliance is undeniable. But his brutal actions, such as his rash and immature destruction of Thebes in 335 BCE, where he razed the conquered city and sold thirty thousand survivors into slavery, or the paranoia that later led to him ordering the execution of loyal companions, serve as warnings against both unchecked power and emotional immaturity. To examine both is to take a more nuanced approach that helps future leaders understand that leadership is complex, rarely perfect, but always transformative. It teaches them that while they can learn from successes, some of the most profound lessons come from navigating failure and prioritizing the human element over purely financial objectives, fostering healing as a team.

"An expert," Nobel Prize–winning physicist Niels Bohr is widely claimed to have said, "is a person who has found out by his own painful experience all the mistakes that one can make in a very narrow field." Leadership education isn't a destination but an ongoing campaign of successes, failures, and learning from both. Just as Alexander continuously adapted his strategies and integrated new perspectives to build and govern his empire, modern leaders must constantly refine their own campaigns by blending analytical rigor with human understanding, fostering resilient teams, and learning from every victory and defeat. A seasoned military commander does not rely solely on ancient maps, after all, but constantly updates them as new intelligence emerges, all the while understanding that every battle, while echoing history, presents its own unique terrain and unforeseen challenges.

Looking Ahead

This chapter has explored how the leader I am today was forged by my background and early experiences combined with continuous learning and direct experience of crisis. Both formal instruction and profound life lessons have been critical to the journey, not just shaping my knowledge and my approach to connecting with people but how I make decisions when everything is on the line.

Yet individual preparation, no matter how profound or thorough, is only one part of the equation for navigating crisis. Alexander's triumphs weren't solely due to his individual brilliance. They were deeply rooted in the strength and unity of his army, his Macedonian phalanxes. In chapter 3, I explore how personal leadership foundations are translated into cultivating unified, disciplined, and loyal teams. Just as Alexander's innovative military formations and the loyalty of his companions were crucial to his success, modern leaders must similarly foster both cohesion and resilience within their own phalanxes.

BUILDING YOUR MACEDONIAN PHALANX

My treasure here lies in myself and my
friends. —Alexander the Great

When I think about Alexander's success, I immediately consider his inner circle of childhood friends who became his generals and governors. These were noble Macedonians whose parents surrounded Alexander's father, King Philip II, and Alexander deliberately chose the most capable individuals from this elite group. This demonstrates a key principle: True merit, even within a preselected elite group, is paramount. Alexander's success was never about one person. It was also about the capable people with whom he surrounded himself, people who had also learned from Aristotle and built upon foundations laid by Philip II and General Parmenion. Alexander was innovative but never threw away the past, instead building on existing knowledge and mentorship.

In my own career, the teams I've assembled have always been built on merit, but they also mirror Alexander's principle of achieving success with the people you started with. For instance, when my company acquired another energy company, I had to decide how to incorporate the other company's departments into my own. I chose to have many of their leaders report directly to me, creating a hybrid leadership team. I wasn't interested in "vanquishing" or discarding the acquired talent; I was interested in integrating them.

By doing so, we retained crucial institutional expertise, and the new people saw that they didn't have to be from "our" culture to win. They realized it was a truly open organization, fostering a shared sense of purpose. This approach proved successful, ultimately leading to a better team. Hiring external experts to come in as "neutral" new faces, as some leaders do in such cases, might seem like a quick fix, but investing in and developing your own loyal and capable team members often yield a superior long-term outcome, even if it initially means a temporary setback. Alexander took the time to incorporate Persians and Indians into his military and government structures, attempting to create a new and improved culture that worked for all of his subjects.

The Macedonian Phalanx: A Philosophy of Unified Action

The Macedonian phalanx was more than just a military formation. It was a profound leadership philosophy. The phalanx revolutionized warfare because, for the first time, an entire group moved and fought as one cohesive unit. Moreover, the phalanx was composed from men ordinarily considered "rabble": the low-status infantry. Under Phillip II, however, the "rabble" became unstoppable thanks to their training and inspiration.

The core idea of the phalanx is that it is only as strong as its weakest link. Individual bravado is replaced by the strength of the unit. A phalanx creates an impenetrable wall of shields and protruding spears, moving as a unit to push the opposition off the battlefield like a tank. As an organizational innovation, the phalanx has taught me invaluable lessons about leadership, unity, and overcoming immense challenges in the chaotic world of modern business.

While earlier forms of the phalanx existed, it was Alexander's father, Philip II of Macedon, followed by Alexander himself, who truly perfected it. Imagine a tight formation where shields were locked together and rows of soldiers were armed with long spears called *sarissas* that extended up and forward, creating an impenetrable wall. This was the first time an infantry group truly moved as a single, unified force, not just in formation, but in combat as well. It was a devastatingly effective technique.

The core lesson embedded in the phalanx is stark: If one soldier drops their shield or breaks rank, it creates a hole that the enemy can exploit and compromises the entire unit. This reality fundamentally shifted the calculus of warfare, placing the unit above the individual, recognizing that collective strength far outweighs any single warrior's prowess.

This military strategy offers a profound analogy for leadership. In my early career, particularly on the trading floor, the culture was often Darwinian, a "survival of the fittest" mentality whereby individuals competed fiercely for personal gain. There was a lot of peacocking, with individual heroes beating their chests. When I became a leader, one of the very first changes I implemented was to move away from this individualistic approach to one based on teams. I wanted to build a phalanx, a single unit where there were no peacocks.

Alexander and his father didn't only understand the unity of the phalanx; they innovated upon it. They realized that merely pushing the enemy off the battlefield wasn't enough: True victory meant annihilating them. They achieved this by combining the immovable force of the phalanx with the speed and maneuverability of cavalry coming in from the wings. The phalanx would push the enemy forward, while the cavalry would circle and envelop them. The method produced incredibly decisive victories at the Battle of Gaugamela in 331 BCE and the Battle of Issus in 333 BCE. Both battles showcased the phalanx's intended role: a disciplined, immovable infantry core that absorbed enemy attacks and held the line, enabling Alexander's cavalry and tactical maneuvers to exploit weakness. To deploy it well required the blend of knowledge, courage, and strength that was Alexander's unique mode of leadership, with all three elements operating together.

Alexander's phalanx principle has deeply influenced how I cultivate loyalty and trust within my teams. It has shown me that genuine loyalty is built through mutual support and shared experiences. Ultimately, the brilliance of the Macedonian phalanx lies not just in its tactical superiority but in its timeless lesson about unity, mutual reliance, and the power of a cohesive unit. It teaches leaders that while individual skill is important, true strength, especially in the face of crisis, comes from fostering an environment where every member understands they are part of an unbreakable wall, ready to move and fight as one. When you know the person next to you is committed to the same cause and you're fighting for each other, it creates an unbreakable bond.

Traits such as integrity and humility are qualities that cannot be taught, which is why I look for them when identifying and developing loyal team members. My goal is to build a "warrior elite," a team that is both mutually supportive and fiercely determined to win, much like Alexander's army. It's a testament to the idea that a group truly committed to each other can withstand any storm, turning potential sites of fracture into formidable bonds.

I have literally used the phalanx analogy with my teams. The concept of "shields locked, moving as one" became a mantra in my trading years. Internally, we could have robust debates and disagreements, but when facing the external world, whether in negotiations or a crisis, we presented a unified face: "one wall," or "one Vistra." To our competitors and our challengers, we were a force to be reckoned with. I drilled the idea that there could be "no holes" in our organization because a single weakness could compromise the entire unit. This disciplined, unified approach ensured that we did all our "fighting" internally beforehand so that when it came time to act, we acted as one.

Inspiring Loyalty and Cultivating Growth

One of Alexander's most impressive capacities was that he did not merely demand obedience, as was his right as a king, but inspired loyalty as a beloved leader. His troops followed him for ten years, through immense hardships. The Gedrosian desert march (325 BCE) was Alexander's punishing return from India, during which thirst, heat, and hunger killed many of his soldiers. The desert crossing was a chance to achieve a feat no conqueror had mastered, not even the famous Persian Cyrus the Great. The soldiers knew it was a dangerous and possibly deadly trek, but they followed Alexander loyally into the desert.

How did Alexander inspire this kind of remarkable loyalty? One key component was what we would today call "management by walking around." Alexander was known for being present with his men, even deep into his ranks, referring to them by name and praising their individual deeds. This personal connection meant so much to those people, and in return, they would, in the words of *The Godfather*, "go to the mattresses" for him. In the Gedrosian desert, Alexander maintained loyalty by sharing hardships with the soldiers, famously refusing water when not enough was available for all, thus bolstering his reputation.

I adopted this principle in my own leadership, walking the trade floor and being present with my teams. I had an office, but I also had a desk right on the trade floor so people could easily approach me. I wanted to build relationships where people trusted me and knew I was invested in them. Because I embedded myself in their everyday workspace, I was visibly and dependably present, encouraging open communication and quick decision-making. I learned early on that it's not being given a title or a rank that makes you a leader; it's the ability to get people to follow you regardless of formal reporting lines. Similarly, in my early career at General Motors, I'd learned that spending time on the manufacturing floor and break room area with the union electricians was important in showing them I wanted to be part of their world. Leaving my office and being present with them developed our relationship, established trust, and ultimately led to higher productivity on my projects by the group.

Alexander's leadership also fostered mutual growth. Many of Alexander's loyal companions, known as the Diadochi, went on to become powerful rulers and governors after Alexander's death. For example, Ptolemy became a king in Egypt and Seleucus ruled in Babylon and other domains. Alexander clearly empowered his team members, preparing them for future leadership roles. Similarly, my "we win together" philosophy evolved a highly individualistic trading environment into a team-centric culture. Our warrior elite had the expectation of winning, but always as a unit. The "we win together" philosophy embodies the idea that success is a collective triumph. It emphasizes teamwork, shared goals, and mutual support, fostering unity within the team. By valuing each member's contribution, this mindset builds trust and resilience, ensuring victories through collaboration, not solitary brilliance. When building my teams, I actively look for individuals with integrity, humility, and ambition because these are foundational traits I cannot teach. In particular, I believe that humility means knowing what you don't know—and then growing from there.

Back in December 2021, the team and I were trying to determine the probability of Russia invading Ukraine, the potential effect on the energy markets, and what we should do about it to protect the company. Many individuals were throwing out theories, some backed by facts and others using historical precedent. As the debate intensified, I noticed that the individuals who demonstrated the most confidence in their theories began gaining ground, independent of the amount of evidence presented. We were working on a problem where the answer was not known with certainty, only based in probabilities. Individual demonstrations of confidence in a theory should not be the leading factor driving action when the information is incomplete. One member of the team was quiet, so I asked them which ideas resonated. The person stated all the things they did not know because of a lack of facts, which was making it hard for them to answer the question. In the process of listing all the things this person didn't know, it turned out the rest of the team didn't know them either. In the process of discovering this, we developed a new theory on how to solve the problem. The exercise encouraged other team members to be more vulnerable in the future and to feel safe in admitting what they didn't know as part of the decision-making process.

Loyalty Under Pressure: Real-World Resilience

The true test of a team's resilience comes during crisis. The loyalty and trust established within my team over years became critical during Winter Storm Uri. Unlike my 9/11 experience, where as a young leader I failed to recognize or know how to handle my team's suffering and ended up marching them to a point where they didn't want to go any further, the Winter Storm Uri response benefited from years of preexisting trust that I had built with my team.

Because Winter Storm Uri happened at a moment of compounding challenge, with COVID-19 restricting movement, our established culture of uniting behind a cause and loyalty to one another meant everyone came in to work the long days necessary. This was not because they were in fear of losing their jobs; instead, it was truly out of a sense of duty to the team, a culture we had grown well before the events in question. Everyone also had permission to go home if they needed to, though few took us up on that. Nonetheless, I myself understood the pull of wanting to be with my own family in a crisis while knowing I was responsible for countless families as everything was going sideways. It was a human approach that acknowledged human needs and desires, and it reinforced my team's loyalty.

Another way I build loyalty well in advance of any crisis is that I take time to identify which team members thrive under pressure and which need support. Using simulated crisis scenarios—for instance, gathering the team and presenting them with a hypothetical crisis, such as, "OPEC just materially cut oil production. What will that do to US natural gas prices?"—I could put each person on the spot, asking them to quickly assess probable impacts and present them in real time. Such stressful exercises reveal who is more likely to handle such a crisis well on their own and who might not do as well without more support in place.

Just as Alexander's success was rooted not only in his individual brilliance but in the strength of his loyal companions and innovative military formations, true leadership in crisis isn't a solo act. A well-constructed team forms the bedrock of crisis response. An effective crisis response takes a symphony of synchronized efforts where each member, nurtured by the leader's consistent development and trust, contributes to a collective force capable of overcoming even the biggest challenges. This type of leadership turns individual strengths into an unbreakable shield, a Macedonian phalanx, against chaos.

The Transition from Individual Contributor to Team Leader

The journey from individual contributor to team leader requires a fundamental shift in focus, from emphasizing personal competency to prioritizing emotional intelligence and shared success. While intelligence and technical skills are essential for excelling as an individual contributor, emotional intelligence is what transforms a competent individual into a respected leader.

Early in my career, as I've mentioned, I observed a *Game of Thrones* mentality in the competitive environment of 1990s trading floors, where individuals hoarded information to survive and to gain advantages. This brutal "survival of the fittest" culture fostered an individualistic approach that constantly pitted traders against one another. When I rose to a leadership position, I consciously moved to change this culture, shifting from individual performance metrics to team-based objectives. This change removed internal competition and allowed my team members to focus their energy externally, on competing with other companies rather than with their colleagues.

Creating a culture where colleagues can be colleagues is crucial. Leaders must be perceived positively by their team members, not just by those above them in the organizational hierarchy. While gaining the respect of superiors may open doors for career advancement, the respect and trust of one's colleagues reveal the true essence of leadership. Leadership only exists where others are not only willing but actually eager to collaborate, follow, and support someone because they see that individual as competent, authentic, and reliable. This kind of lateral influence, built on credibility and mutual respect, often speaks louder than titles or promotions. Observant leaders look for those who have this kind of respect, and who attract and retain followers, even if they do not yet have a leadership title to go with it. It is the foundation of effective teamwork and sustainable leadership.

My "we win together" philosophy is intrinsically linked to the concept of the Macedonian phalanx. The phalanx, with its interlocking shields and unified movement, symbolized a unit greater than the sum of its parts, where individual bravado was subordinated for the sake of collective strength. When I shared about Alexander with my teams, I also cultivated a mindset akin to top-tier sports programs, where championship performance is the norm. Such high expectations, while motivating, also meant that severe losses, such as Winter Storm Uri, hit extra hard—as we'll discuss later in the book. The greater the track record of success, the more profound the emotional impact of significant failure. This experience taught me the delicate balance of pushing for greatness while simultaneously understanding the human toll of crises and setbacks and acknowledging that leaders and teams must process and recover from losses.

The *Trading Places* Philosophy

One of my all-time favorite movies is the classic *Trading Places*, starring Eddie Murphy and Dan Aykroyd. I've always loved the way it blends sharp social commentary with humor and heart, but more than that, it's been a surprisingly effective tool in my leadership playbook. When I needed to motivate my team and align everyone around a common, tangible goal, I would often turn to a memorable scene from that film—the one at the very end, where Billy Ray and Louis are relaxing on a tropical beach, drinks in hand, having made their fortune. That image became a metaphor I used regularly: a symbol of what success could look like for all of us if we played our cards right as members of a unified team.

I would often tell my team, only half-jokingly, that their personal goal should be "to get rich." Even in a capitalist system, that kind of directness can feel a little jarring, but I meant it sincerely. If *they* got rich, it meant our shareholders got *really* rich. That's how value creation works in a commercial enterprise. Our specific organization was the "tip of the spear," the sharp edge that drove growth, profit, and results. We operated within the guardrails of ethical business conduct and legal compliance (and safety first!), but we were also unapologetically driven by outcomes. When the outcomes were good, everyone benefited. But it took the whole team to make it happen.

This analogy wasn't just a quirky nod to an old movie; it was a way of answering the unspoken question every team member eventually asks: "What's in it for me?" By painting a vivid and humorous picture of the financial upside, I made our collective goal concrete, aspirational, and a little fun too. It made people feel like they weren't just working hard for the benefit of a faceless corporation; they were building their own futures.

I'm fully aware that not everyone is wired this way. Some people are drawn to mission-driven work or seek fulfillment through service, mentorship, or innovation. Those values are equally vital, and individuals who prioritize them have essential roles to play throughout any great company. But within the commercial part of the business, the part I led, our mission was profit. We were honest about that, and we didn't try to dress it up as something else. When I was clear and even a little cheeky about our purpose, I found it actually galvanized the team. People felt empowered to chase results, and they understood that their success was directly tied to their effort.

In short, *Trading Places* wasn't just a favorite film; it also became a shorthand for what my team and I were building together. It was my way of saying, "If we do this right as a team, if we stay focused on our shared purpose and play to win, we all get to sail off into the sunset someday."

Bringing People Along on Your Journey

A cornerstone of my leadership philosophy has always been the long-term investment in people, not just as professionals, but as human beings with potential, loyalty, and their own growth trajectories. I've never believed in treating team members as disposable or interchangeable assets, and I've intentionally pushed back against the conventional wisdom that says you should swap out employees when the business landscape shifts or as new skill sets become more relevant. I've chosen to stick with the people who have been in the trenches with me, even when it might have been easier or more expedient to bring in fresh talent. That decision, while not always easy, has been one of the most rewarding of my career.

There's something deeply powerful about choosing to believe in your people not just because of who they are today, but for who they can *become.* I've seen firsthand how this kind of long-term commitment fosters loyalty, trust, and a strong sense of purpose. People perform differently when they know their leader is in it with them for the long haul. They show up more fully, more bravely, and more creatively because they know they're being invested in, not evaluated for the next round of cuts.

Building that kind of cohesive team isn't a quick process. In my experience, it takes three to five years, at minimum, to discover whether a group of individuals will truly "gel." It's like building a professional baseball team: You don't just chase the flashiest talent or the highest-paid free agents (unless you're the Yankees or the Dodgers). Instead, you build a roster with balance. You draft and develop players who fill roles, who complement each other, and who contribute to the team's chemistry and resilience. That means when someone hits a slump—and everyone hits slumps sometimes, even MVPs—the others can carry the load without blame or panic. That's what trust looks like in action. It's a "no person left behind" mentality, not unlike the ethos of the Marine Corps. When Winter Storm Uri hit and the world shut down, I watched in awe as members of my team risked their own safety to make sure our operations didn't fail. That kind of sacrifice doesn't happen in highly transactional corporate cultures. It only happens in teams where people know they are seen, valued, and protected.

One way I've honored that commitment to development is through mentoring. I actively invest in people by assigning stretch assignments, trusting them with responsibilities beyond their current scope, and challenging them to rise. I do this because it was done for me. Some of my greatest career milestones came because someone bet on me before I was technically "ready." Now, I pay that forward. I believe the best leaders are those who create opportunities for others to grow alongside them, not just behind them. Over time, this builds an inner circle like Alexander's, a close-knit crew of experienced professionals who are not only highly capable but deeply loyal because they know you believe in them not just as employees but as future leaders in their own right.

This approach is radically different from many traditional corporate models. In many companies, the go-to move is to "buy the best," plug them into a role, and expect immediate results. It's a short-term play that prioritizes speed and capability over cohesion. It might deliver quick wins, but it also breeds anxiety, creates internal competition, and undermines trust. People start looking over their shoulders, wondering if they'll be the next to be replaced by a so-called superstar hire.

My approach leans in the opposite direction. I believe in building a team that is meant to last, a true phalanx. I want teams that function as resilient, interdependent ecosystems. The teams I build don't flinch when the environment changes because they've already weathered storms together.

That was never more evident than during Winter Storm Uri. The crisis rendered every rule book we'd ever worked from obsolete. But because the team had already built high internal trust during other difficult moments, we adapted quickly. We coordinated across agencies, utilities, and political entities with a level of agility that simply wouldn't have been possible in a less cohesive team. What emerged was something bigger than strategy, a real shift in mindset. We stopped thinking like a for-profit entity and started thinking like human beings trying to protect each other and the people of our state. During an unprecedented winter weather emergency, our work wasn't about the market anymore. It was about survival.

The experience of navigating Winter Storm Uri was a stark contrast to what I lived through during 9/11. Back in 2001, I learned the painful lesson that if you ignore the emotional toll of a crisis, you risk a breakdown in trust and, eventually, mutiny. That's why, when Winter Storm Uri hit, I told my team, "Take care of your families first. We'll figure out the rest." That single statement reshaped the emotional tone of our entire response. People gave everything they had not because they were forced to, but because they felt safe, supported, and seen as human beings.

This emphasis on compassion, vulnerability, and psychological well-being is what sets my leadership style apart. While others double down on performance metrics, I invest in emotional maturity and the capacity to navigate failure with grace. That's what leadership actually is—not perfection but presence and intention. Not control but care. As a result, my metaphorical baseball team doesn't just win an awful lot of games; we've played the game together so long, we can pull off a 6-4-3 double play without having to think about it.

Loyalty Under Pressure

Strong teams exhibit recognizable behaviors when they're under pressure, and I've learned that the quality of a team is most evident not during a period of calm but when everything starts to unravel. In the moments when millions of Texans were thrown into chaos—power outages, collapsing infrastructure, and freezing temperatures, with the grid minutes from total failure—what kept the team moving forward wasn't a flawless strategy or cutting-edge technology but the strength of our team's culture. The loyalty, trust, and cohesion we had built over years revealed themselves in real time. Most of the team gave up a significant portion of their Valentine's Day on a moment's notice, spending it at the office helping the state get ready for Winter Storm Uri, which was forecast to hit early the next morning. I was very proud of their commitment to the state and the company, but even more proud of their commitment to each other's success.

This didn't happen by accident. The deep trust among team members we relied on during the storm came from years of battling adversity together, both personally and professionally. Recall that the Winter Storm Uri crisis didn't occur in isolation; it happened in the middle of the COVID-19 pandemic, before vaccines were widely available. That meant we were fighting two invisible enemies at once: the storm outside and the virus inside. But even with threats on both sides, I saw the power of culture.

In those moments, I reminded the team, "The state needs us." It wasn't just about keeping the business afloat; it was about stepping into a larger purpose. They responded brilliantly, not because they had to, but because they wanted to. People came into the office, working around the clock, fueled on pots of coffee and vending machine food, sometimes even removing their masks when urgency outweighed everything else. I didn't demand that level of commitment—my team volunteered it. That level of loyalty wouldn't have existed in a remote team thrown together or among individuals who hadn't shared past hardship. Peer pressure played a role too, but in the healthiest sense, as a collective commitment, with space and grace for those with health concerns who couldn't join in person.

One of the most important things I was able to give my team during Winter Storm Uri wasn't a solution but permission. I told them they had the "pocket ace" of walking away if it became too much. The reassurance of knowing there would be no punishment for stepping back freed them to lean in fully. It eliminated hesitation, cleared the mental clutter, and allowed us to take decisive actions, sometimes encouraging us to step out of our comfort zones.

Leadership also means knowing who you want in your foxhole when the bullets start flying. I've spent years observing how people react under a range of real and hypothetical scenarios—Macedonian troops and historical battles, today's conflict in Ukraine, cyberattacks on infrastructure, gas shortages, and more. These exercises reveal who performs under pressure—who can think clearly, communicate fast, and act decisively. They're the ones who rise to the occasion when the situation crumbles. But you can't identify them by résumé alone. You must watch them move in and through uncertainty, and you, as the leader, must stay composed enough to see clearly through the fog.

Operating without a full dataset has become the norm in the business world, not the exception. My background in engineering trained me to lean on logic and analysis, but when I shifted into trading, I learned the hard way that crises don't wait for complete information. In those moments, you must combine what you *know* with what you *sense*.

Alexander the Great knew this well. During the Battle of Gaugamela in 331 BCE, he faced a Persian force that vastly outnumbered his own. On paper, he should have lost. But Alexander's troops had trained relentlessly under him. He trusted their flexibility and courage because he had led from the front, not the rear. When the Persians flanked his right, Alexander didn't wait. He pivoted, broke formation, and personally led a cavalry charge through the enemy lines, straight toward the Persian king, Darius. That pivotal battle moment shattered the Persians' cohesion. But it only worked because Alexander's men trusted him completely; they had rehearsed the art of improvisation in real-world battle conditions and were fully prepared to follow an unorthodox plan. That's what I mean by muscle memory, by a culture forged in fire. Alexander's victory at Gaugamela wasn't just a function of strategy; it was a function of trust and rapid execution under extreme pressure. That's the same spirit we had to channel during Winter Storm Uri.

Learning Through Failure

I've come to see that true leadership is ultimately defined by growth, learning, and healing. It definitely is not about a smooth, polished narrative of unbroken success. Instead, it's about being honest enough with yourself—and for my part, with my readers—to admit where you've failed and being vulnerable enough to share the cost of those failures. What I've lived, the hardships I've faced, the missteps I've made, and the emotional scars I've carried have shaped me far more than any title or achievement ever could. This isn't a success story in the conventional sense. It's a testimony of failing forward, of recovering, of learning the hard way what real leadership costs.

When I reflect on history's great leaders, I find value not only in their triumphs but in their flaws. Obviously, Alexander the Great stands out as a brilliant figure, yet he was also a deeply complicated one. His paranoia drove him to execute some of his most loyal companions. Philotas and Parmenion, both trusted generals, were killed under charges of conspiracy that many historians consider dubious. Tragically, Alexander also murdered Cleitus the Black, a man who had saved Alexander's life in battle but whom Alexander stabbed in a drunken fury after Cleitus criticized his decisions. These isolated acts of rage created fractures within Alexander's inner circle, eroded trust, and ultimately alienated many of his Macedonian officers. When Alexander began elevating himself above his men, insisting on *proskynesis*—ritual prostration—and on being worshipped as a god, it signaled a dangerous descent into self-isolation.

For Alexander the Great, the wake-up call that could've saved him from himself didn't arrive. Mine did. My own painful wake-up call after 9/11 forms a central theme of this book: We learn as much, if not more, from our lowest points as we do from our greatest achievements. Not only that—we can learn not just from our own mistakes but also from the errors of those who came before us.

Leadership is not a static skill. It's a constantly evolving practice, a craft shaped by lived experience, humility, and reflection. My "education" has not only taken the forms of formal training and management frameworks. I've had to stand in the trenches of the chaos of real life and figure out, sometimes in hindsight, how to do better the next time.

To me, leadership during crisis is a lot like navigating a white water river. At first, it's all adrenaline—you're paddling hard, reacting fast, using your strength and instinct to keep the raft afloat. But as you gain experience, you learn that true mastery isn't just about making it through the rapids. It's about understanding the currents, anticipating what's around the bend, looking out for rocks below the surface, and most importantly, knowing when to pull ashore. You have to check on your team, patch the raft, maybe take a break and recharge. If you ignore the signs of fatigue or you cling to a broken paddle out of pride, you're not a leader—you're a liability. I've capsized before, and every time I did, I learned something that helped me navigate the next set of rapids more wisely.

The lesson of this chapter is one of the most crucial I've learned: Strength through unity is the bedrock of crisis leadership, and unity in turn is born of trust, respect, and shared history. That type of bond doesn't appear overnight. You earn it. You build it one decision at a time and by being present, remembering people's names, and honoring their sacrifices.

In his earlier years, Alexander understood this. His generals and companions weren't just subordinates but childhood friends, fellow students of Aristotle, men who had grown up with him. They marched with Alexander for over a decade, enduring brutal conditions to help build one of the greatest empires in history. Even when they reached their breaking point at the Hyphasis River, their refusal to continue wasn't rebellion but exhaustion. Alexander's men were loyal to him because he led from the front, because he bled with them, because he recognized their deeds and rewarded their courage. This idea of being embedded with your people is something I've tried to embody ever since 9/11. It's not enough to manage from the top down. You have to lead shoulder to shoulder, shield to shield, especially when the stakes are high.

Building a resilient team also means building one that is diverse not only demographically but intellectually and emotionally. Alexander, for all his flaws, intuitively grasped this. Despite his teacher

Aristotle's belief in Greek superiority, Alexander famously adopted Persian customs and incorporated local leaders into his imperial administration. He wasn't afraid to challenge the norms of his time to build a more integrated, and thus more sustainable, empire. I've taken a similar approach in my own career. When we acquired another energy company, as I mentioned earlier, I didn't regard it as a takeover but an opportunity to join forces. I knew what was needed was a hybrid leadership team, one that combined our companies' strengths and preserved institutional knowledge. Creating this team respected what the other company brought to the table—there were reasons why my company acquired them, after all!—and we forged something stronger together.

I don't measure my success by titles or bonuses—I measure it by the careers I've helped build. The greatest compliment I ever received is watching my people thrive. Some of my direct reports have been with me for twenty years. I've seen them rise, evolve, lead others, and even retire. That kind of longevity and loyalty from an inner circle doesn't happen by accident. It only happens because you invest in people, challenge and mentor them, and create a culture where winning together matters more than individual glory.

Alexander did this too. Many of his generals, the Diadochi, went on to become powerful rulers in their own right. Ptolemy, Seleucus, and Antigonus weren't just followers; they were leaders Alexander had developed and empowered. The legacy of a true leader is not measured by how brightly that leader shines but by how many others they've helped illuminate.

Ultimately, team resilience after failure emerges when that team acts like a loyal, well-drilled military unit. While individual prowess is important, unwavering commitment to the unit, mutual trust between people, and adaptive leadership that knows when to push and when to protect its members are all the more so. These are the things that allow a team to absorb the shock of defeat, learn, and march forward into new territories, their phalanx stronger than before.

Looking Ahead

As we move forward, we will transition from the internal dynamics of team cohesion to the external realm of strategic readiness. In our next chapter, we'll explore the critical moment when preparation meets chaos, detailing how rapid adaptation becomes a necessity for leaders and their well-forged teams when reality defies even the most meticulous planning. Knowing that the strength of your phalanx can carry you through the unforeseen is one part of being prepared to "cross any Hellespont." Strategic readiness is the other.

CROSSING THE HELLESPONT

Remember, upon the conduct of each depends the fate of all. —Alexander the Great

The Hellespont, that narrow but storied strait separating Europe from Asia, was never just a strip of water to Alexander the Great. For him, it was the ultimate threshold—a dividing line between the known world and a campaign whose outcome no one could predict. Standing on the shore, Alexander was not merely preparing his troops to march into Persia. He was committing them, body and soul, to a venture that would either immortalize them forever or destroy them. Crossing meant leaving behind the security of home and the comfort of the familiar and stepping into a storm of uncertainty with no guarantee of return.

Alexander treated the crossing with ritual weight. Later Greco-Roman writers recorded that he paused to make sacrifices to Poseidon and the Nereids, casting offerings into the water and symbolically binding his destiny to forces larger than himself. These actions were not just a matter of religion; they were a deliberate sign of leadership. His soldiers needed to see that their king did not hesitate or question but instead embraced destiny with open arms. The Hellespont became more than geography—it became a psychological point of no return for Alexander and his men.

For modern leaders, the phrase "crossing the Hellespont" serves as a metaphor for that moment when preparation collides with the unknown. No matter how carefully leaders forecast, reality will break the script. The crisis may come earlier than expected, with greater ferocity, or in forms no one imagined. At that juncture, plans become secondary to personal resolve. Leaders discover that their true job is not to enforce a plan but to embody steadiness when others waver. It is precisely here—where the existing playbook does not have all the answers—that crisis leadership begins.

Alexander's Battle Adaptability: Calling the Audible

Alexander's genius was not that he carried a flawless master plan into every engagement but rather that he possessed the rare judgment to know when a plan had reached its limit and should be reconsidered. His leadership was built on a remarkable equilibrium of preparation and improvisation. Unlike commanders who clung to rigid strategies, Alexander understood that the battlefield was alive, unpredictable, and merciless to hesitation. His education under Aristotle gave him more than philosophy—it gave him a worldview shaped by adaptability, reasoned analysis, and the courage to recognize emerging patterns amid apparent chaos. That training in observation and logic prepared him to pivot with confidence in moments when others froze, unsure of what to do. For Alexander, flexibility was not a weakness; it was the ultimate strength of a leader who knew how to blend intellect with instinct.

Take, for example, the Battle of the Granicus, Alexander's very first major encounter with the Persian empire. By every account, it was a moment where the campaign could have ended before it had truly begun. The Persians had positioned their forces in strength along the steep banks of the river, waiting for the Macedonian army to attempt a slow, vulnerable crossing. Any textbook general of the time would have paused, probed for weaknesses, or waited to find more favorable ground. That was conventional wisdom, and to follow it would have been considered a wise course. Yet Alexander was not satisfied with convention. He studied the terrain, gauged the psychology of both his men and the enemy, and then chose to seize the initiative rather than surrender it. In a single decisive command, he ordered his cavalry to charge headlong across the river and strike directly at the Persian line. The decision was reckless by the standards of traditional generals, but precisely because it was reckless, it achieved the important element of surprise. What seemed like folly instead became brilliance in execution. Alexander's men, galvanized and inspired by his audacity and leadership, transformed disadvantage into advantage, uncertainty into momentum, and momentum into morale and success! That victory at the Granicus River was more than tactical; it was symbolic of Alexander's entire approach to leadership—bold, adaptive, and utterly unwilling to be trapped by tradition.

What makes this instinct strikingly modern is how directly it applies beyond the battlefield. In business, in government, and in military command today, leaders are constantly tempted to cling to strategies long after conditions have shifted. They want the comfort of the plan, even when the plan is visibly failing. A neatly designed strategy provides psychological safety, but it can become a trap if followed blindly. I learned that during my 9/11 experiences. I was trying to pursue our financial position without truly understanding that everything had changed in the span of a horrifying morning and I needed to lead an entirely new way.

Alexander's example demonstrates that true leadership rests not in dogged adherence to a failing path but in the willingness to adjust course in real time. The most effective leaders understand that adaptability is not the opposite of decisiveness—it is decisiveness in its highest form. A quarterback who changes the play at the line of scrimmage is not being indecisive. They are reading the defense, recognizing the moment, and calling an audible—changing to a new play on the basis of spur-of-the-moment verbal instructions—to maximize their team's chances of success. Great leaders in every field live in the space of balancing preparation with improvisation and long-term vision with immediate action. They know that leadership is not about proving the plan right but about ensuring that the mission succeeds, even if that means cutting through the knot of tradition to carve out a new path.

When Crisis Strikes Unexpectedly: Winter Storm Uri

We have each faced our own personal Hellespont—the narrow, uncertain crossing between what we know and what lies ahead. Each of us has been there. It can be personal, such as leaving a relationship or making an intensely felt choice, or it can mean pushing forward in a professional setting where we face difficult forces. I am no exception. My career has brought me to moments where the map quite literally ended, where the familiar scaffolding of preparation dissolved, the storm arrived without warning, and leadership was tested in the raw immediacy of real time. Of all these trials, the most painful and unforgettable came with the onset of Winter Storm Uri, a disaster that pressed leaders across Texas into choices few could have imagined. The storm's ferocity exceeded every model and projection. Like the monster that was Hurricane Katrina, there really was no precedent for what we were facing. Systems that had been tested and had held over decades began to unravel within hours. The thin margin for error, always a precarious balance in the energy sector, evaporated entirely. Suddenly, millions of people across Texas depended on our decisions, on our ability to respond faster than the collapse unfolding before us. In such moments, the weight of responsibility ceases to be a metaphor. It becomes almost physical—a heaviness that settles deep on the chest, pressing down until every breath feels deliberate, measured, purposeful. Even the most seasoned leaders, men and women who have weathered years of professional storms, can feel the first tremors of paralysis ripple through their bodies. It is the fight-or-flight response made real, in real time. When the brain becomes flooded with uncertainty, it instinctively reaches for denial. The first whispered thought is always, *This cannot be happening—not like this, not to us, not now.*

Yet reality does not wait for disbelief to run its course—life does not work that way. It charges ahead, indifferent and unyielding, stacking failure upon failure until the situation feels unbearable.

Winter Storm Uri delivered those cascading blows with ruthless precision. Gas prices, which my team and I had assumed would stabilize at $20 per unit, did not inch upward—they skyrocketed. They vaulted past $200 and then $300, numbers so far beyond any contingency that even the most pessimistic of planners had never allowed them into the conversation. The prices were in the realm of "unimaginable." Infrastructure, stressed by freezing temperatures and surging demand, cracked and splintered in ways that our shelves of binders full of contingency plans had never envisioned. The neat, careful outlines crafted in boardrooms were exposed as powerless when measured against the brutal chaos of reality—and this unprecedented storm. There was no playbook for a disaster of this magnitude, no checklist or manual that could restore order. Every system bent toward collapse, and with each new crack came the temptation to panic, to wait for someone else, somewhere else, to have the answer.

I had felt this before. During 9/11, as a young and inexperienced leader, I had been caught in that paralysis. I waited for guidance, believing that *surely*, someone higher up, someone older, someone who had endured more, someone with more leadership and a *plan* would step in with a way forward. But the hard truth was that no one came. In crisis, there is rarely someone else with more certainty. That memory came roaring back during Winter Storm Uri, nearly twenty years later. And this time I understood with sharp clarity: No one else was coming. I was the one in charge. The burden—and the privilege—of leadership was mine. The responsibility to project calm, to coordinate action, and to set the rhythm for hundreds of people rested squarely on my shoulders. That realization, frightening as it was, stripped away hesitation. Clarity emerged because I frankly had no other choice.

Decisions had to be made with half-formed data because waiting for certainty was equivalent to failure. We improvised endlessly: patching systems with tools never designed for the task, rerouting supply lines on the fly, buying minutes where we desperately needed hours. Each fragile success was temporary, but every temporary fix bought us just enough time to keep the larger structure intact. With every hour survived, the team discovered new reserves of resilience, new ways to push through exhaustion.

Momentum became our lifeline. It was never elegant—often chaotic, always imperfect—but it kept us moving. And movement itself became the victory. What mattered most was that, much like Alexander's men, we did not stall, did not break, did not allow the enormity of the storm to strip us of our will. When stability finally began to return, I looked around and realized we had endured something that defied description. The fact that we were still standing was not the triumph of flawless planning or the product of any neat operational or organizational chart. It was a triumph of human resilience, of collective endurance against impossible odds, of teamwork and solidarity.

The lesson seared itself into my memory. Leadership in crisis is not about possessing perfect foresight or flawless strategies. I had learned that during 9/11, but I truly lived it during Winter Storm Uri. Leadership in crisis is about becoming a hinge that does not snap when everything else swings wildly out of control. Your team must absorb shock after shock without suffering collapse. True crisis leadership is not about elegance—if you had seen us after being mostly awake for days, I promise you, *elegant* is not the word you'd have used!—it is about resilience. It is not the comfort of prediction but the courage of conviction. This kind of leadership means standing in the center of the chaos, rallying people to act as one body, and pressing forward even when every logical voice says *retreat*. Above all, leadership is the relentless faith that when the ground falls away beneath your feet, you will step forward anyway, hold the line, and carry others with you until stability, however fragile, returns. This, in turn, calls to mind our Macedonian phalanx.

When Planning Fails: The Siege of Tyre and Beyond

What do you do when every plan fails? When no precedent exists and the challenge before you seems impossible? That is when leadership is most starkly revealed.

Alexander faced this dilemma at the Siege of Tyre in 332 BCE. The city stood on an island, fortified by walls that plunged straight into the sea, guarded by a fleet that dominated the surrounding waters. Every conventional military tactic was useless. For many generals, such a scenario meant stalemate or retreat, certain failure.

Alexander refused that idea. His solution was audacious: He ordered the construction of a half-mile causeway across open water. It was less a battle plan than an engineering marvel. For seven months, his men labored, hauling stone and timber into the sea, slowly extending a road toward the city. Tyrian ships harassed the effort constantly, forcing Alexander to improvise defenses, adjust construction methods, and even create floating siege towers to shield workers. What began as an unprecedented challenge became a continuous contest of innovation, where every move by the enemy demanded a countermove from Alexander.

The siege of Tyre illustrates one of the purest lessons in crisis leadership: When traditional paths collapse, invention is the only way forward. Leaders cannot cling to pride of authorship, insisting on their original ideas. They must be willing to discard what no longer works and embrace radical new approaches. In Tyre, Alexander demonstrated that persistence, creativity, and adaptability together can crack even the most impregnable fortress.

For modern leaders, Tyre is a parable. Whether in technology, healthcare, finance, or public policy, we often face fortresses of our own—problems with no historical solution. Success does not come from repeating old formulas. Instead, leaders must try what has never been attempted in order to forge a path forward.

The first decisions a leader makes in a crisis shape everything that follows. In the opening hours, there is no excuse of exhaustion or attrition. Eyes are on the leader, morale is fragile, and momentum is undecided. Those initial moves either instill confidence or sow despair. Bold clarity sets a tone and a standard that cascade through the entire organization, while hesitation spreads as rapidly and destructively as a fire.

Crisis leadership, then, is not only about solving problems but also about projecting steadiness when uncertainty reigns. People can withstand extraordinary hardship if they believe their leader is clear-eyed, competent, and decisive. They falter when they sense a leader wavering.

Looking Ahead

As we move into chapter 5, "The Gordian Strategy," we will explore the effect of leadership style during a crisis more deeply. Some challenges cannot be unraveled strand by strand; they must be cut through with bold, unconventional choices. Where chapter 4 has shown the necessity of adaptation, chapter 5 will show the necessity of decisive, even radical action. It is in that combination of adaptability and audacity that the essence of leadership in crisis is truly found. The next chapter will illustrate how leaders, faced with seemingly intractable problems, can forge new paths by embracing calculated risks. We will uncover the power of swift, strategic decisions to transform chaos into opportunity. Ultimately, chapter 5 argues that true leadership lies in the courage to act, sometimes with incomplete information, when the stakes are highest.

PART II

INTO THE FIRE:
CONFRONTING
CRISIS

THE GORDIAN STRATEGY

*In the end, when it's all over, all that matters is
what you've done. –Alexander the Great*

In the relentless fire (or blizzard!) of a crisis, when time evaporates and the stakes rise to seemingly impossible heights, leaders often find themselves confronted with problems that resist every conventional solution. These are not the ordinary challenges that yield to careful step-by-step analysis or patient incremental effort. They are moments when the pressure is so intense that hesitation itself becomes as dangerous as the crisis. In these situations, the difference between success and failure, between survival and collapse, can rest entirely on a leader's willingness to act.

Such crises are defined by their refusal to fit within old frameworks. Traditional playbooks, the comfortable reliance on precedent, and the security of slow consensus all fail under the weight of urgent necessity. A leader cannot afford to endlessly weigh options ("analysis paralysis"), debate subtleties, or cling to the rules of the past. Each passing moment erodes the margin of safety. Hesitation invites chaos. To linger in analysis is to squander the few opportunities that remain.

True leadership in these defining moments requires courage of a different sort: the courage to break free of convention, to abandon the predictable, and to embrace boldness in its purest form. The essence of decisive leadership under pressure is not recklessness but clarity—recognition that the crisis demands an unconventional solution and that delay will only deepen the danger. Bold decisions, made swiftly and with conviction, can cut through complexity like a blade, transforming what appears impossible into a breakthrough.

This chapter centers on the art of courageous leadership when under extreme pressure. It demonstrates how, in certain rare and defining moments, the only path forward lies in shattering the assumptions that govern ordinary decision-making. The Gordian strategy is not about rashness but about daring to see beyond traditional approaches and trusting in the power of decisive action. By stepping outside the boundaries of convention, a leader can turn paralysis into momentum, fear into confidence, and crisis into opportunity.

The Alexander Principle: Cutting the Knot

The ancient legend of Alexander the Great and the Gordian knot offers one of history's most enduring metaphors for decisive leadership and the willingness to defy convention when the stakes demand it. In the city of Gordion, in the very heart of Phrygia, an old wagon sat in the public square, its yoke bound by a knot so complex and tightly wound that it defied explanation. Some claimed King Midas himself had tied it, others King Gordius, and still others said it was tied by the gods, but its real origin was unknown. The prophecy attached to it was simple yet immense in its implications: Whoever could unravel the knot would be destined to rule all of Asia. Generations of ambitious men had tried and failed. Some tugged gently, hoping patience would reveal a hidden thread. Others attacked it with brute strength, muscles straining in vain as the cords tightened further with every pull. The knot itself became a symbol of human limitation, an insoluble riddle mocking both persistence and ingenuity.

When Alexander arrived at Gordion in 333 BCE, the challenge was placed before him. Here stood not just a physical puzzle but a cultural test. Tradition dictated that the conqueror attempt to work the knot slowly and reverently, honoring the sacred ritual. To fail would not be shameful—after all, countless others had failed—but to succeed would crown him with legitimacy and divine approval. Yet Alexander was not interested in ritual for its own sake. He was not a man who valued slow unraveling when momentum mattered more. With his army restless and the weight of an empire pressing him forward, Alexander made a choice that would forever mark his reputation. Instead of fumbling with cords, he drew his sword and, in one swift stroke, cut the knot in half.

The act was shocking. We can imagine that onlookers gasped and the public square filled with murmurings. Some surely thought him reckless, even sacrilegious. The knot was not just a puzzle—it was sacred, a relic bound up with prophecy and the gods. To desecrate it was to court the wrath of the divine. Yet Alexander's action reframed the entire narrative in an instant. By refusing to be bound by convention, he demonstrated something far more important than cleverness: his absolute resolve. He showed that he would not allow himself, his army, or his destiny to be shackled by the past. According to later Greco-Roman writers, that very night, a thunderstorm rolled across the skies, and Alexander's followers took it as Zeus's own affirmation of the deed. Whether it was providence or coincidence, the thunderstorm confirmed in the minds of many that Alexander had indeed been chosen for greatness. His solution not only solved the immediate challenge but also broadcast a profound message to allies and enemies alike: This was not a man who would be slowed by tradition. He was prepared to defy precedent, shatter expectations, and impose his will in pursuit of victory.

I think of a movie scene that many of us are familiar with. In the classic *Raiders of the Lost Ark,* Indiana Jones is faced with a menacing swordsman, yet it appears all he has is his bullwhip. However, our hero takes a decidedly Gordian knot approach, produces a pistol, and shoots the swordsman unexpectedly.

For modern leaders, the Gordian knot endures because it captures a timeless truth. Not every problem can be solved by patience, process, or adherence to tradition. Some challenges must be cut through with a clarity and boldness that unsettles those around us. The Gordian knot reminds us that certain problems are not meant to be unraveled strand by strand. They demand decisive severing.

Modern Application: When Convention Fails

Just as Alexander faced the Gordian knot, modern leaders confront moments where conventional methods collapse in real time. I encountered precisely such a moment during Winter Storm Uri, when the foundations of the Texas energy system were strained to the breaking point.

At the outset, we attempted to respond conventionally. My team of energy traders did what they had been trained to do—analyze risks, calculate costs, arrange for fuel, understand power plant capabilities, and anticipate customer consumption. But the storm mocked these efforts. Gas prices, which in ordinary conditions hover between $2 and $4 per unit, began to rise at frightening speed. Within hours, they had leapt to $20 (where, as I wrote in the previous chapter, I assumed they would stay, since until that point, that price had been a virtually unheard-of upper limit). Then the unthinkable figure began to spiral higher and higher. The prices eventually rose to $400 per unit.

The same thing happened with customer consumption of electricity. Consumption went up far higher and far faster than any of the models predicted. Power plants were struggling to keep up with customer demand. Some of them tripped offline while trying to ramp up fast enough to meet the surging demand, putting more pressure on the remaining plants. We were watching increasing demand creating strain that reduced supply at the very moment power was needed the most. It was a domino effect that resulted in ERCOT, the grid operator, shedding power demand on the system and placing a large percentage of the state in the dark in order to save the power grid from total collapse. Power plants can only generate a certain quantity of electricity in a given amount of time. When the demand for power exceeds the ability to create power in that time period, something called *frequency on the system* begins to drop. When the frequency drops too low, power plants begin to trip offline. This is what happened in the opening moments of Winter Storm Uri as it started to pound Texas.

We didn't have *time* to wait for prices or grid conditions to settle down. Hesitation meant disaster. Every moment spent arguing with the math was a moment of the grid edging closer to collapse. Without decisive and targeted gas purchases, plants would shut down, pipelines would stall, and millions of Texans would be left freezing in their homes. The paradox of leadership was stark: The very principles we prized—prudence, fiscal responsibility, risk aversion—now stood in direct conflict with our higher responsibility to protect human life.

As the storm progressed, I knew the decision had to be reframed. I gathered my team and told them plainly, "People are dying. Our responsibility is to prevent the grid from collapsing further. If we overpay today and prices fall tomorrow, that failure rests on me. I take full accountability. Your job now is to act without hesitation."

In that moment, by shouldering the responsibility personally, I freed them from fear of career-ending mistakes. Accountability became the sword that cut our own Gordian knot.

But financial decisions were only the beginning. Convention failed everywhere. We rapidly built coalitions across boundaries that normally divided us. Competitors who once jealously guarded information began cooperating with each other. We coordinated with natural gas producers, natural gas processors, electric utilities, and pipeline operators—entities that are not accustomed to collaborating directly. The power market in Texas is deregulated; market prices send signals to the various market participants who, in turn, make the economic decisions that serve to keep the system in balance at the minimum cost. This framework works very well in Texas and has served as a model for the rest of the country. Winter Storm Uri was testing this market in unpredictable ways. Market mechanisms alone were not enough to solve all the problems associated with a power grid in partial collapse. We needed to coordinate more closely with other industry participants and the state government. We improvised a set of communications protocols, independent of market price signals. If a power plant needed gas, the pipeline operator told us the best place and producer to buy it from. If a gas producer needed power to restore frozen wells, we talked with the electric utility and got them to restore power to the wells by moving power from somewhere else. The objective was to restart gas production at strategic locations on the gas pipelines in order to maximize the amount of production at each power plant. The problem was no longer to determine the lowest possible cost to generate the power needed to serve customer demand. The challenge was to maximize generation at all costs and strategically prioritize the restoration of energy infrastructure where it would make the biggest impact. It was messy, inefficient, and entirely unconventional—but it was movement, and in crisis, movement is survival.

Fresh thinking emerged from unexpected quarters. Our CFO made a suggestion that changed the course of our response at a specific power plant. He suggested we bring in experienced operators from New England, people accustomed to subzero temperatures, who knew how to handle frozen equipment. This outside perspective, simple yet brilliant, smashed through paralysis. We flew our New England colleagues in on a private jet for speed and then had to drive them for two hours on frozen roads to get to the plant. Soon, that plant was producing more power. The suggestion was inspirational.

The financial toll was staggering. In a single week, our company absorbed more than $2 billion in losses. But the alternative—complete grid failure—would have been apocalyptic. Water systems would have failed. Roads already blocked by ice would have become impassable. Hospitals could have shut down. Families would have faced weeks without heat. The death toll would have dwarfed what we ultimately endured. In the calculus of crisis, paying unthinkable monetary prices and coordinating across different entities in unconventional ways became the only moral choice.

Like Alexander at Gordion, we realized that convention was a luxury we could not afford. Tradition, procedure, and precedent all had their place, but they could not save lives in those desperate hours. The only path forward was to cut through the Gordian knot with decisive clarity, to embrace unconventional alliances, and to act with relentless resolve.

This lesson endures: Leadership is not always about unraveling problems patiently. Sometimes, the world presents us with knots too tangled for traditional solutions. In those moments, the only option is to take up the sword—figuratively or literally—cut through the paralysis, and lead with conviction, no matter the risk.

Shadow Side: Boldness Versus Recklessness

There is a razor-thin line between boldness and recklessness. Alexander's decision at Gordion, like many of his daring charges against Darius the Great, worked. But unchecked boldness can be ruinous. The darker side of Alexander's character—his explosive temper and impulsive violence—is exemplified by his tragic murder of Cleitus the Black, a loyal general, in a drunken rage. One decisive stroke of the sword wins an empire; another destroys trust and loyalty forever.

Modern leaders, too, must distinguish between courageous decision-making and destructive impulsivity. The difference lies in preparation and principle. Boldness must rest on a foundation of guiding values, clear priorities, and a disciplined framework for risk.

In Winter Storm Uri, my decisions were bold, but they were anchored in one principle: Saving lives outweighed every other consideration.

Organizations can prepare for moments of extreme uncertainty by creating decision hierarchies or a set of guiding principles well before a crisis ever arrives. These should be formalized, but they are not meant to be rigid playbooks or overdone manuals destined to collect dust on a shelf. Instead, they should be living frameworks that rank priorities, clarify boundaries, and establish predefined risk thresholds. A well-constructed set of guiding principles provides leaders with the equivalent of a navigational map in stormy seas: It doesn't remove the turbulence, but it does consistently point toward true north. Quick frameworks, such as three-step escalation protocols, priority matrices, or crisis response hierarchies, give decision-makers a mental structure to fall back on when adrenaline and fear threaten to overwhelm judgment. Predefined guiding principles remind leaders of what matters most when time is short: protecting people, preserving trust, and stabilizing the system. Risk thresholds, meanwhile, function as "red lines" that prevent reckless improvisation. For example, a hospital may preestablish what resources it is willing to divert during an emergency surge, or an energy company may define the maximum load it will shed to protect the grid from total collapse. These thresholds help teams act swiftly without overstepping into panic-driven choices.

The goal is not to dampen boldness or suppress innovation. Rather, it is to channel courage into a usable form. In high-pressure situations, boldness without direction can quickly devolve into chaos, just as hesitation without clarity can paralyze. Guiding principles create guardrails strong enough to prevent catastrophic errors but flexible enough to allow leaders to seize fleeting opportunities. This balance between structure and agility is what separates resilient organizations from those that unravel in the face of shock.

When courage is channeled, it becomes constructive rather than destructive. A leader guided by a clear decision framework knows that decisive action can be taken without betraying the organization's values or abandoning its mission. In this way, boldness is not a gamble but a disciplined form of leadership under pressure.

Looking Ahead

Decisive action, such as cutting through the Gordian knot, is only the first step in a crisis. In the initial hours, bold moves buy time, stop the bleeding, and reframe the problem. But crises rarely end in a single stroke. Once the immediate emergency has been stabilized, the true challenge begins: the long, grueling work of coordination, resource management, and sustained endurance.

Leadership shifts from rapid-fire decisions to orchestrating large systems under strain. What began as a sprint quickly becomes a marathon. In the next chapter, we will examine how leaders must transition from the urgency of immediate action to the patience of prolonged command, building order from chaos and sustaining morale through the long night of crisis.

CREATING ORDER FROM CHAOS

With the right attitude, self-imposed limitations
vanish. —Alexander the Great

The brutal Texas wind was a stark contrast to the warmth February usually carries. Texans, like most people across the country, often take the rhythm of the weather for granted. By February in Texas, winter is usually giving its final gasp, and there is a soft promise of spring in the air. But there was no promise in this wind. It slashed across the landscape like a scythe, harsh and merciless, cutting to the bone and rattling windows as though determined to remind us all how fragile comfort really is ... and not to take the weather for granted!

My mind, normally a well-oiled machine of calculations, contingencies, and instinctive strategies, felt locked inside its own prison of ice. The patterns and probabilities that usually hummed smoothly in my thoughts stuttered now, frozen by the enormity of the disaster unfolding in the form of Winter Storm Uri. The Texas energy grid was failing spectacularly and terrifyingly, a failure without precedent in modern memory.

The phone calls that crashed into my ear were full of panic. Each brought a fragment of catastrophe. There was no good news. Power plants were tripping offline. Natural gas pipelines were losing pressure in the relentless freeze. Gas production was being curtailed as wells and gas production equipment either lost power or froze. Temperatures plummeted to levels no one in Texas had truly prepared for, turning homes into iceboxes and highways into graveyards. Every update painted the same portrait: a system unraveling thread by thread, faster than any one team could possibly reweave. Each voice on the line carried a mixture of urgency, panic, and disbelief, seasoned professionals choking on words they had never expected to say out loud.

On the trade floor and in our emergency operations center, it seemed as though every alarm had been triggered at once. Monitors displayed the crisis as it happened, while phones rang in overlapping choruses. This was not a crisis that could be solved by flipping to page 17 of a manual. This was something else entirely, an existential threat that demanded innovation in real time, improvisation in the face of odds that bordered on impossible.

I let my eyes scan the room, taking in the faces of my team. Men and women who had stood through difficult days before and had faced their share of strain and complexity now wore expressions of exhaustion, disbelief, and fear. The weight of the moment hung visibly on their shoulders. In an instant of clarity, I understood something that sent a chill through me colder than the storm outside: This was my team's battle. There were few others to look to. There wasn't anyone above me to whom I could pass the decision. Unlike 9/11, when I had been a younger vice president, caught in the shock of an unthinkable tragedy and waiting for direction that never truly came, I was now the executive vice president in charge of the commercial team. By definition, the buck stopped squarely with me.

I had to set the course.

At that moment, I did not realize how my past had been preparing me for this crucible. As a team, we needed to make order out of chaos. I had learned—sometimes painfully—that in moments like these, decisiveness and speed mattered more than perfection. To hesitate was to invite catastrophe to spread. The lesson carved into me by earlier crises was clear: Leaders must act, even without perfect knowledge, because the cost of delay is measured not only in dollars or reputations but sometimes in lives.

In the suffocating weight of that chaos, when the roar of crisis threatened to drown out every rational thought, my mind reached almost instinctively back across centuries to the example of another leader who had stared down a world in disarray: Alexander the Great. History remembers him as a conqueror, a general who extended his empire from Greece to the edges of India. But to me, in that moment, he was something more: a man who understood that conquest was only the beginning of leadership. Alexander's genius was not only in winning battles with brilliance and daring but in shaping what came *after* the dust of war settled. He was not merely a taker of territories but an inventor and builder of systems, one who cleverly blended cultures. In short, he was a ruler who grasped that true leadership extended far beyond the battlefield.

Alexander knew what many leaders never learn: Winning a war is only half the struggle. The harder part is taking the rubble of conquest and shaping it into a coherent structure that can endure. Alexander understood the delicate art of weaving disparate peoples into a single fabric. He imposed order, building not just an empire but a vision of unity that outlived him to the extent that we speak of his accomplishments and his leadership even today. In that dark winter, staring down a storm that threatened the stability of millions of lives, I could not help but see the ancient truth that victory is not survival alone. True leadership means creating order, no matter the chaos that threatens to consume us.

Alexander's Administrative Genius: From Conquest to Cohesion

Alexander's campaigns dazzled with military brilliance, but his leadership shone just as much in the aftermath of victory. Imagine the challenge of taking control of vast geographies populated by diverse peoples with their own religions, loyalties, and customs. Many leaders might have imposed their own people as governors, stripping away local leadership in favor of familiar loyalists. But Alexander understood something deeper: Lasting control would not come from domination alone. Enduring stability required integration. Successful empires demand the creative construction of a new order that fits a new situation, not just forcing an old order onto a new bit of the map.

One of Alexander's most telling moves came after defeating Darius and claiming the Persian empire. Rather than purging the Persian leadership wholesale, Alexander deliberately retained certain Persian nobles in significant administrative roles. This was not weakness or leniency but strategy. By keeping experienced leaders in place, Alexander leveraged their knowledge of the local governance, customs, and people. These nobles knew the intricate machinery of Persian administration, and Alexander recognized that their cooperation was far more valuable than their submission. Stability was better served by pragmatic inclusion than by sweeping replacement.

Equally important was Alexander's deliberate adoption of Persian dress and customs. Some of his Macedonian officers found it offensive, even scandalous. But Alexander knew that symbolism carried power. By inserting himself into Persian traditions, he sent a message: He was not merely a conqueror ruling from the outside but a ruler willing to respect, and even embody, the culture of his new subjects. This was not empty theater; it was deliberately calculated to knit two worlds together—diplomacy on a grand, comprehensive scale.

Alexander recognized that empires cannot be held for long by force alone. They require a structure, symbols, and systems that give people a reason—whether practical or emotional—to accept a new reality. He was not just a warrior charging into battle. He was an architect of stability who designed systems strong enough to outlast his presence.

This blend of intellectual preparation and practical strength created a framework for effective crisis leadership. Centuries later, I tried to channel the same principle in Texas when the grid shuddered under Winter Storm Uri.

Modern Application: Forging Functional Systems in Texas's Darkest Hour

At first glance, comparing Alexander's empire and our struggle during Winter Storm Uri might seem a stretch. After all, we were not conquering nations. We were engaged in a different kind of survival, fighting to hold together the critical infrastructure of a state when natural forces seemed determined to tear it apart. But like Alexander, we needed a profound shift in mindset to succeed: moving from competitive silos to systemic cooperation, from independent decision-making to integrated responses.

The immediate crisis centered on natural gas. Texas power plants depend heavily on it, but as temperatures plummeted and demand for heat skyrocketed, gas production froze—literally. The price of gas, usually a few dollars a unit, soared into the hundreds. My team hesitated. They were good people, trained to make sound financial decisions and loyal to the principle of fiscal responsibility. But the market had collapsed into a state of distortion for which no training manual had ever prepared them.

It was then that I overrode the bedrock principle of business—profit. "People will die in this catastrophe," I told my team. "We have to make sure the grid doesn't get any worse."

I called my CEO and explained matter-of-factly that we would lose money. At the time, we thought it might be tens of millions, perhaps even a hundred million or more. We were way off. For Vistra alone, the losses eventually totaled more than $2 billion. But people's survival mattered more than a company's balance sheets. I removed that fiscal responsibility burden from my team's shoulders: "This is on me. Buy the gas. Get the units up. Don't worry about your jobs. Don't worry about the money." Doing so unlocked the capacity for decisive action.

Order began to form amid the chaos, this single decision starting a cascade of change. We began using what we called the "bread analogy." Before Winter Storm Uri, every part of the supply chain—bread bakers, truckers, grocery stores, and consumers—functioned independently. And when disaster struck, the shelves became empty. After the storm, the approach shifted. Bread bakers stocked raw materials, trucking companies winterized their fleets, stores prepared emergency reserves, and individual families kept extra loaves in the freezer. The difference wasn't just a matter of individual preparation; it was coordinated, system-wide resilience.

Even our competitors recognized the shift. Kinder Morgan, a major pipeline infrastructure company, reached out, asking not how to profit, but how to help. "This is greater than profits," they admitted.

Instead of exploitation, Kinder Morgan offered collaboration. They coordinated with us on the best place to buy gas to mitigate the fuel shortage at one of our power plants. This coordination ended up extending to the gas producer, the gas processor, the gas pipeline, the power plant, and the electric utility, all working together to deliver the power to the appropriate customers. Collaboration became essential.

Government oversight transformed too. Where regulators had once taken a hands-off stance on many issues, Winter Storm Uri forged a new reality. Now, inspections are stricter, winterization is mandated, and communication flows faster and more openly.

We built work streams that focused on technology and communication. Technology concentrated on building better systems for real-time data and management reporting so we could make better decisions with more information. Communication efforts focused on bringing more decision-makers from across different areas to the table and sharing information more broadly with public relations and public policy personnel. The broader communication with a steady cadence has made it easier for internal personnel to communicate with external stakeholders during a crisis.

The Shadow Side: The Human Cost of Chaos

Creating order comes at a price. Every decision carried a psychological weight. The fear of failure, of financial ruin, of lives lost, was constant. I felt it. Every single member of the team felt it. Even Alexander had moments when his composure cracked. No leader is invincible.

I first learned this lesson during 9/11. As a younger executive, I pushed my team too hard, blind to their trauma, focused only on results. They disengaged, worn down by grief and exhaustion. That failure haunted me for years. Winter Storm Uri gave me a chance to lead differently. I prioritized the human side, offering people permission to go home and trusting my team members to make the decisions that were right for them and their families. Tellingly, many stayed at work, driven by a fear of missing out on being part of the solution.

I also relied on my lieutenants. One kept me grounded, checking on my health, lightening the mood, even debating me when necessary. The other was unflappable, calm in the storm, signaling when it was time to pause and think. Their balance anchored me. Every leader needs both kinds of support—those who challenge and those who steady.

Looking Ahead

Order is not established once and for all. It must be maintained, adapted, and hardened against the next storm. Alexander's legacy lasted because he thought beyond battle. Winter Storm Uri's legacy must be the same. Any crisis your company faces must bring about change and improved processes.

In the energy sector, new playbooks now exist for gas pipelines, emergency drills, and coordination between public and private sectors. Competitors have learned that rivalry takes a back seat when survival is on the line. Regulators understand that oversight must be consistent and focused. And leaders know that waiting for order is not enough: It must be actively forged.

In that frozen week, we did more than keep the lights on. We laid a foundation for resilience. We showed that leadership in crisis is measured not by what we endure but by the systems we build that last beyond the storm. From the dust of ancient Persia to the ice of modern Texas, the lesson is the same: True leadership is creating lasting order from chaos.

COUNTING THE COST

I will not steal my victory. —Alexander the Great

The immediate confrontation phase of Winter Storm Uri was over. The frantic scramble, the desperate calls, and the emergency decisions made in the middle of the night had all passed. But in its truest and most enduring sense, the crisis had only just begun. During the storm itself, the mission was visceral and straightforward: Keep the lights on, keep people alive, keep the system from collapsing in the relentless storm. The simplicity was brutal, and as a result, our purpose was clear. We abandoned the familiar economic objectives because, in those hours, we weren't running a company—we were fighting to generate power and save lives. Reliability was our creed. If we failed to deliver electricity, if we failed to stabilize the grid, we knew what the consequences would be. The financial debates would have to wait until after the storm.

For us, during Winter Storm Uri, once the adrenaline receded, the roar of alarms quieted, and we clawed back enough capacity to keep the grid from crumbling, a darker, colder phase arrived. This was the *reckoning*—the moment when leaders step out of the trenches, triage the wounded, and confront the aftermath.

We had survived the unthinkable. I believe millions still had power because of the effort we all made. Yet a haunting question hung in the air: *At what cost?* The shift from running on instinct during battle to performing the accounting of the costs is perhaps the most defining and painful passage in leadership. It is where the warrior becomes the steward of war's consequences. It can be numbing.

I dedicated my career to studying disruption, preparing myself over decades by analyzing historic market crashes, researching the campaigns of Alexander the Great, and synthesizing the wisdom of philosophers and generals alike. I believed I understood risk and loss, thinking my experience during 9/11 had toughened me against shock. Yet nothing—not a classroom, nor a trading floor, nor even the trauma of watching the towers fall—prepared me for the hollow, gut-wrenching sensation of seeing the power grid nearly collapse, millions of dollars vanish hourly, and tens of millions of lives severely disrupted by the unfolding tragedy, knowing each moment that power to millions of homes and the financial future of the company hinged directly on the decisions we were making.

At first, the numbers looked survivable. Early estimates placed the financial damage at around $500 million. That figure, enormous as it was, already felt like a mountain dropped on our shoulders. Considering how horrible the crisis had been, it was almost expected. In the frantic pace of the confrontation phase, the financial costs were background noise. What mattered was keeping the grid from crashing. But soon, as the storm stretched on, gas prices skyrocketed, and every plant decision rippled into escalating costs, the full scope became horrifyingly clear. We weren't talking about hundreds of millions anymore. We were staring into the abyss of billions. There was no walking that back. We were hemorrhaging at a rate that seemed impossible—millions of dollars every hour, gone. It was like watching blood drain from a body, knowing that without the transfusion of decisive leadership, the entire system would bleed out.

The End of the Old Metrics

In "normal" times, business success in the energy world is measured by four cardinal principles: safety, adherence to environmental rules, reliability, and profitability. They form a kind of compass, guiding operational and strategic decisions. But Winter Storm Uri forced us to reorder that compass in ways no one could have imagined.

Safety remained immovable, untouchable—we would never, could never, ask a plant to run in a way that put people in danger. But environmental constraints became negotiable in that moment. Waivers were requested, not to disregard the environment permanently, but because production had to be maximized in the short term. Most radical of all, the objective of making money—the fourth principle of our business—was an extremely distant consideration to reliability and safety.

I told my team, in words that have since been quoted back to me many times, "Buy all the gas." Don't worry about price. Don't hesitate because it looks outrageous. Don't stop to calculate margins. Buy whatever it takes to keep the units running. The crisis had long since outgrown profit and loss considerations. The team needed to do what was necessary, regardless of whether accountants or investors would ever forgive the cost.

What struck me most, in hindsight, was the void that opened up once the financial objective evaporated. In business, profit is both a measure of success and a motivator that provides focus and direction. When you strip it away, when you accept that you are burning billions of dollars with no chance of recovery, the intensity that fuels the fight to make money fades, leaving something different in its place. For me, that *something* became people—a crusade to keep hospitals lit, to keep families warm, to prevent Texas from descending into total darkness. That noble purpose steadied me. It became a cause greater than the spreadsheets, worth every sleepless night and every harrowing choice.

The Weight of Leadership in Isolation

The scale of the financial hole was almost impossible to comprehend, even for the most senior leaders. I watched the strain etch itself across the faces of our CEO and CFO. They could not hide the stress, and I didn't expect them to. My CEO, in particular, wanted desperately to reassure people, to tell them, "All is calm." But the truth was, he didn't yet have all the numbers, and those he did have pointed in the opposite direction. It was anything *but* calm. He was constrained by lawyers, by accountants, by the delicate dance of public messaging. The burden of caution weighed heavily on him.

Meanwhile, I had no such luxury. The daily responsibility of making decisions and judgment calls fell squarely on me. It became *my show*; everything had my name on it. The burden of command isolation is immense. In those moments, you realize, in a way you never had before, that no matter the hierarchy, no matter the corporate chart, no matter how reliable your people or how supportive your lieutenants are, when the chaos is on top of you, the leader on the ground carries a tremendous weight.

The Investigation and the Power of Transparency

The instant the physical crisis of Winter Storm Uri began to subside, the cruel inevitability of the next battlefront arose: investigation. The shift was abrupt. One moment we were consumed with the sheer mechanics of survival: keeping turbines running, securing every available molecule of gas, and preventing cascading blackouts across the grid. The next, we were catapulted into a wholly different battlefield, one defined by regulatory requests, legal filings, and the slow grind of external scrutiny. For a public company, an event of this magnitude is just not something that can be wrapped up in an internal memo and saved for the next quarterly earnings call. The scale of the financial loss was so extraordinary, so immediate, that it triggered a mandatory disclosure to the market—an 8-K filing. That single document placed us squarely under the microscope of both state regulators and shareholder investigators.

This phase was deeply unsettling; in many ways, it was more unnerving than the storm itself. During the crisis, adrenaline carried us forward. There was no time to doubt, no room to hesitate; there was only action. But once the lights were back on and homes were warm again, our exhausted team, who had given every ounce of themselves for days without sleep, now found themselves in the peculiar position of facing judgment.

Two emotions dominated the atmosphere in those first days of inquiry: anger and anxiety. Anger rose up because the very people who had poured their strength and ingenuity into saving the grid now felt as though they were being treated as suspects rather than saviors. Anxiety seeped in because they feared that outsiders—people who had not lived through the nightmare minute by minute—would misinterpret their actions, second-guess their motives, and cast blame with the cold clarity of hindsight.

I had lived through this kind of postcrisis scrutiny before, in the chaotic aftermath of 9/11. The lessons had been painful. Back then, I discovered the hard way that secrecy or hesitation in the face of investigation only deepens suspicion and erodes trust. That experience seared into me the necessity of what I now call *radical transparency*. It was with that principle in mind that we made one of our smartest decisions: Even before the storm reached its crescendo, we embedded a lawyer into our core team. While engineers and operators battled frozen valves, while traders scoured the market for scarce gas supplies, this attorney documented, in meticulous detail, every single decision, every trade, every operational adjustment. He counseled us in real time on the legal implications of our choices, even as those choices were being made under extreme duress. I often watched him, head bent over his notes, face drawn with tension, as he tried to keep pace with the dual reality we were living: a life-and-death fight to preserve the grid in the present and the inevitable questioning that awaited us in the future.

When the official investigations began, there was a deep sense of fear and frustration within the team. They were concerned about the ramifications on any second-guessing of their decisions. People were asking themselves, *Could I have made a better decision in that moment with the information I had? Will they understand that we did our best? Will that be enough?*

My directive to the team was blunt and absolute: *Stop. Give them everything.* We had nothing to hide. I had been present for every minute of the ordeal, had witnessed the decisions my people made, and I trusted them. I wanted the investigators to see the nightmare as it truly was and to experience, as much as possible, the impossible conditions under which we had operated. They needed to understand that our choices were guided not by speculation, calculation, or profit but by a singular principle: the safety and stability of the grid and of the people of Texas.

That decision to embrace full transparency was the right one. As the process unfolded, the investigators, regulators, and shareholder representatives combed through mountains of records—emails, trading logs, operational directives, handwritten notes from the control room. Their conclusions were unambiguous. Every action we had taken, from buying overpriced gas at jaw-dropping rates to carefully pushing plants to their designed limits, had been done out of necessity. Not once did they find evidence of greed, deception, or negligence. Instead, they saw professionals making impossible choices in impossible circumstances, continually guided by integrity.

By choosing radical transparency, we turned accountability into a shield. We proved that when ethics anchor decision-making—even in the darkest, least predictable, most confusing hours—an organization can withstand the fiercest scrutiny. Transparency, in the end, was not just a legal strategy. It was a deliberate, consciously chosen ethical stance, and it was the reason our team survived intact.

Responsibility Versus Blame

The investigation forced me to pause and clearly articulate something that often gets blurred in the heat of postcrisis reflection: the difference between responsibility and blame. This is foundational, not just a subtle nuance. I needed my team to grasp this principle too, because without it, the stress of scrutiny would have fractured us. I told them plainly that, as the leader, I carried the full weight of responsibility for everything that happened under my command. Every decision that was made, every action taken, and every outcome—whether it brought praise or disaster—ultimately rested on my shoulders. That, I reminded them, was nonnegotiable. Leadership does not allow for convenient disclaimers or selective ownership. You cannot enjoy the authority without also accepting the accountability. But responsibility is not synonymous with blame. That distinction mattered more than ever.

Blame belongs to the person who betrays trust, someone who acts unethically, who knowingly violates stated principles, or who chooses deception over honesty. Any of these actions corrode the very foundation of any team.

Honest mistakes, on the other hand, even costly ones, are the inevitable byproduct of human beings making split-second decisions under enormous pressure. I tell my people that when someone chooses what they believe to be the best course of action with incomplete information or under impossible constraints, and it does not have the desired results, that mistake is not theirs to bear alone. Such mistakes are shared burdens. We carry them collectively, and we learn from them together. The battlefield of leadership is filled with imperfect choices. No one should be punished for choosing wrongly when their intent was rooted in integrity and commitment.

Dishonesty is another matter, a line I draw with absolute firmness. If someone lies, if they attempt to cover up a mistake or mislead their teammates, it's a deal-breaker, no matter how brilliant, talented, or indispensable that person might seem. Lies do more damage than any operational error. A single falsehood can unravel the trust that holds an organization together, replacing solidarity with suspicion and fear. No amount of skill can compensate for the rot of dishonesty. Talent without integrity is a liability, not an asset. I was unequivocal and unambiguous on this point; everyone knew where the boundaries lay, and everyone understood that truth was our first defense.

This clarity became our shield against the corrosive and extremely common culture of finger-pointing. When things go wrong, the blame game can become the default mode in many organizations. Leaders deflect responsibility downward, peers turn against one another, and individuals scramble to protect themselves by shifting fault elsewhere. It becomes a toxic and insidious spiral, destroying morale, eroding loyalty, and making recovery nearly impossible. By defining responsibility as mine but blame as conditional upon ethical failure, I cut that cycle off before it could begin. My team did not waste energy on self-protection or internal rivalries. Instead, we stood shoulder to shoulder—our version of the Macedonian phalanx—owning the totality of our response as one.

What emerged from that moment was not a culture of fear but a culture of resilience. By refusing to indulge in finger-pointing, blame-hunting, and backstabbing, we built trust. By separating responsibility from blame, we preserved dignity. By insisting on honesty as our immovable cornerstone, we created a foundation strong enough to withstand not only the storm but also the relentless spotlight of investigation. In the end, it was not our perfection that carried us through but our commitment to truth, shared ownership, and the unbreakable bond of collective responsibility.

Segmenting Communication and Managing Trauma

The aftermath did not have equal effects on everyone. I led teams across twenty different states, and their reactions reflected their unique experiences.

The Texas team was understandably devastated. This group lived through the worst of the storm. They were exhausted, traumatized, and grieving. Their lives were intertwined with the suffering all around them. For them, the message was simple: *I am in the same boat with you. It's OK to be devastated. We will admit mistakes, cooperate fully with investigations, and fight to protect both the company and Texas.*

Teams outside Texas felt the shock differently. Their questions were financial and existential: *Does this mean the year is lost? Does my work even matter? Will this $2 billion hole erase my contributions? (And my chance at a bonus?!)* For them, the message had to be different: I had to provide them with reassurance, guidance, and a reminder that their work still counted. I promised them that their efforts would be recognized and rewarded, even if the company was battered.

This dual-track communication was critical. Without it, the anxiety of some and the trauma of others could have fused into a paralyzing culture of despair.

Wisdom over Bravado

Winter Storm Uri transformed me in ways I never could have predicted. When I was thirty, during 9/11, I carried myself with a bold confidence and unshakable ambition. I thought I was invincible, fueled by adrenaline and a naive certainty that intensity alone could conquer any challenge. I equated leadership with charging harder, pushing further, and proving my worth through fire and determination. To me, victory was the result of domination and sheer force of will. But as earnest and driven as that version of myself was, I lacked the wisdom that only time, scars, and responsibility can build into a leader's worldview.

Alexander, too, evolved as he passed through the crucible of experience. In his earliest campaigns, he was reckless, driven by conquest, glory, and an insatiable hunger to demonstrate that he could live up to his father's legacy. He needed to prove himself worthy of the favor of the gods. He relentlessly sought battle, viewing each confrontation as an opportunity to prove himself. Yet as he grew older, his leadership shifted. He recognized that being a ruler required more than victory on the battlefield; it required vision. Alexander began integrating cultures, adopting local customs, and embracing new traditions that would bind diverse peoples into something resembling stability. The sword gave way to diplomacy, and the reckless charge yielded to calculated endurance. This was not a loss of power but a maturation of it.

Similarly, I have come to value wisdom over bravado. The storms of life—whether literal, like Winter Storm Uri, or symbolic, like 9/11—strip away illusions. They force a reckoning with what truly matters and who you are deep down. Leadership is not about sprinting toward every fight or seeking constant opportunities to prove dominance. It is not about being the most aggressive and loudest voice in the room or the most relentless in pursuit of conquest. Instead, it is about discernment, knowing which battles are worth waging and which should be declined.

The question I now carry into every decision-making process is no longer, *How do we win?* That feels shallow, even dangerous, to me now. A better, deeper question is, *Does this have to be a fight?* Can resilience, trust, and stability be built another way—through collaboration, endurance, or simply the courage and patience to wait out the storm without losing faith?

The true legacy of crisis leadership is not perfection. Perfection is a mirage, something leaders chase when they are young and desperate to validate themselves. The true legacy of crisis leadership is resilience, surviving with integrity intact; it is about coming through the fire without compromising the values that define who you are. The triumph is not found in the absence of scars but in the fact that we endured, stood firm in the face of devastation, and upheld our principles even when it would have been easier to cut corners or abandon them.

For me, the measure of success with regard to Winter Storm Uri was not in profit margins or performance metrics. The success was that we endured as a team, that we did not fracture under pressure, and that we emerged with lessons profound enough to guide the next generation. The younger version of me would have thought only of conquest, of leaving behind a trail of victories. But the older, experienced version of me knows that the greatest inheritance I can offer is not a story of domination but a road map of resilience.

I went through the nightmare. I bore the reckoning, shouldered the weight of responsibility when there was no one else to carry it, and came out the other side with an understanding of leadership far richer than any textbook, seminar, or theory could ever teach. Uri was a storm that broke me, but in that breaking, something stronger was forged. Leadership, I learned, is not about proving yourself immortal in the heat of a particular battle—it is about guiding others safely through it, no matter how battered you become in the process. To me, that is the truest definition of victory.

Looking Ahead

The chaos has subsided, the grid has stabilized, the immediate fire of confrontation is behind us, and we have met the painful necessity of counting the cost. The aftermath can be the most critical phase of leadership, but it is often the least discussed. Financial and professional loss carries an immense personal burden in the form of exhaustion, professional failure, and shame. As leaders, we are forced to pivot from prioritizing economic objectives to prioritizing human lives, an unassailable and ethical purpose. Yet the psychological weight of the tremendous costs remains and demands answers.

To move beyond it, the emotional debris must be confronted. This is the focus of the beginning of Part III: The Indus Principle: Into New Territories. The next chapter, aptly titled "It's Not Your Fault," further addresses the critical distinction between responsibility and blame. The wisdom gained from surviving profound challenges becomes the foundation for future leadership. As we step out of the shadows of crisis, we experience a necessary evolution in our approach. The final phase of the journey demonstrates how transforming painful lessons into resilient systems and protocols enables us to develop a more nuanced understanding of success, thereby building a leadership legacy that extends far beyond immediate crises.

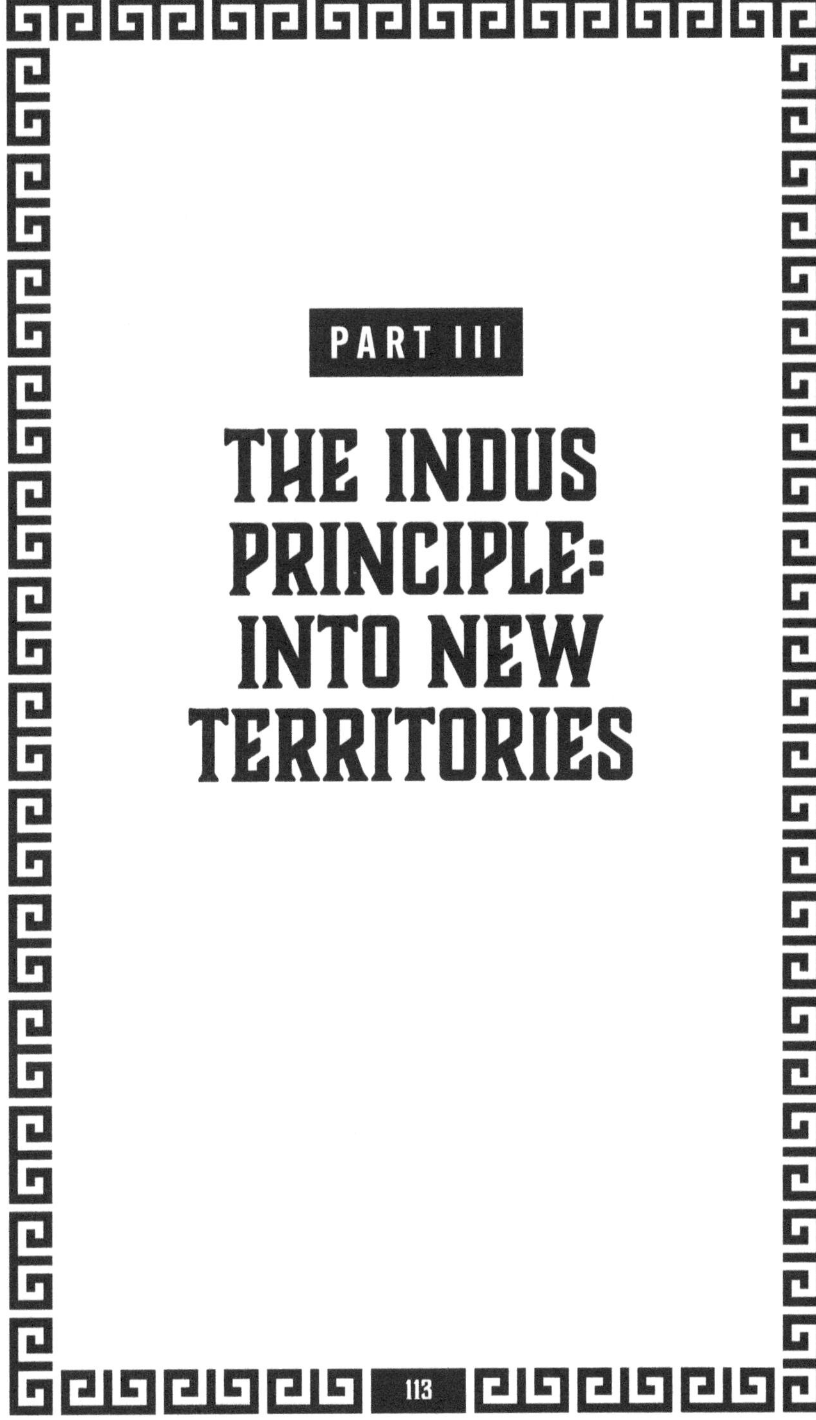

PART III

THE INDUS
PRINCIPLE:
INTO NEW
TERRITORIES

IT'S NOT YOUR FAULT

Whatever possession we gain by our sword cannot be
sure or lasting, but the love gained by kindness and
moderation is certain and durable. –Alexander the Great

The smoke had cleared. The lights were back on. The immediate crisis
of Winter Storm Uri, the most devastating event of my professional
career, was technically over. Yet as the generators wound down and
the hum of power returned, a deeper silence settled in, one far heavier
than the blanket of the thick storm itself. The adrenaline that had
fueled me for days began to drain from my body, leaving a hollow
ache in its place. The physical storm was behind us, but the real
battle—the invisible one, the crisis of the soul—was just beginning.

For days, I had been running on fumes, sustained not by rest
or reason but by sheer will and a lot of coffee—to be honest, I'm
still not sure what fueled us all. In the midst of chaos, adrenaline
becomes your armor and your substitute for food, sleep, and coherent

thought. You shift into triage mode, operating on instinct and muscle memory. Every moment is consumed by logistics: who's got power, who's gone dark, where the next problem is likely to flare up. Your world contracts into a sequence of urgent decisions, a high-stakes game of Whac-A-Mole.

My team was fantastic. My personal Hephaestion—a renowned general who was among Alexander's closest lifelong friends—was Aden, a grounding force inside the storm. Then there were voices like that of another close advisor on my team, Claudia—someone slightly removed from the event itself who could remind me there was still a world beyond the crisis.

Once the noise dies down and the lights are steady again, an eerie quiet sets in. There's a strange exhaustion as the adrenaline dissipates. That's when the isolation of command really hits. It's exhaustion on an existential level. You've been surrounded by people nonstop, then suddenly, you are alone. The adrenaline that protected you abandons you, and what's left is a raw confrontation with yourself.

Now, for the first time, I realized I had no one to talk to who could fully understand the weight of what had just happened. I didn't need to complain or seek sympathy. Whining would have trivialized the magnitude of what we endured. But I did need to process that I'd been through something extraordinary and acknowledge the psychological debris leadership leaves behind when the crisis ends. When everyone looks to you for steadiness, where do you take your own tremors? Who carries the leader when the leader is trying to carry everyone else? Or afterward?

This chapter is dedicated to that fragile, often unseen terrain—the emotional aftermath that follows survival. It is about learning to navigate the thin lines between responsibility and blame, guilt and growth. As a leader, I know that responsibility means owning the outcomes and the decisions. I also know that blame can fester and turn toxic. The distinction between responsibility and blame matters profoundly because, without it, the crisis never really ends; it only migrates inward, metastasizing into self-doubt or shame. True healing, for a leader, begins when you can face the darkness that remains within you after the lights are back on. This is the work of recovery, of rediscovering integrity when everything feels burned-out and brittle. It's how you begin to rebuild not only the systems you manage but the self that was tested in the fire.

The Core Principle: Responsibility Versus Blame

From 9/11 to Winter Storm Uri, each catastrophe left scars. In time, these scars would become a map for my leadership going forward. This book's underlying architecture is built on the premise that crises reveal truth about people, systems, and above all, leadership. Most leadership literature celebrates vision, strategy, and innovation, but rarely does it confront the emotional and moral weight that comes with being "the one in charge" when everything goes wrong, or that slippery difference between responsibility and blame. This lack was one of my major motivators for writing this book.

I believe without hesitation that in the end, you—the leader—are responsible for everything. Every decision, every misstep, every success, every failure, every word spoken by your team traces back to your influence. Leadership is ownership, period. This means that responsibility begins not with what happens externally but with self-reflection: You either built the team, or you inherited it and chose to keep it. Either way, it's yours. After a reasonable transition period—say, six months—you can no longer point backward to your predecessor or sideways to your peers. By then, the team's culture, rhythm, and results belong to you. You own the tone, the tempo, and the trust within your organization. Responsibility is not merely managerial; it's moral. It's the silent ethical contract you sign the day you accept the title of leader: that you will carry the full weight of outcomes, even those you didn't directly cause.

If responsibility encompasses everything, though, where does blame fit in? Blame, to me, is far narrower and darker. I reserve it for acts of deliberate deception, conscious sabotage, or unethical behavior. Blame can and should be assigned when someone lies, hides information, manipulates data, or acts in bad faith. Those are misdeeds and breaches of trust, not just mistakes. Outside of deceit or malice, though, leadership must live in the realm of responsibility, not blame.

The difference may sound semantic, but it defines entire cultures. Responsibility drives growth, reflection, and accountability. Blame breeds fear, silence, and paralysis. When things go wrong—and they inevitably will—the instinct to find a scapegoat is powerful. The corporate bloodstream floods with defensiveness, narratives form, and people scramble to rewrite history to protect themselves. But true leaders resist that gravitational pull. They stop the finger-pointing and turn the lens inward: *What did I miss? What systems failed on my watch? What tone did I set that made this possible?*

A culture of blame is the easiest refuge in a moment of failure. It gives the illusion of control, a way to make the chaos feel contained by naming a culprit. But that illusion is poison. Once blame takes root, learning stops. People start managing appearances instead of outcomes, protecting themselves instead of the mission. A strong leader must fight that impulse every single time it occurs, especially when pressure is at its highest. It's too easy to point fingers at the traders, the engineers, or the dispatchers who were "closest to the problem." But the truth is, the responsibility is located higher. A true leader recognizes that responsibility, by definition, cannot be delegated. You can delegate tasks, authority, and accountability but never responsibility.

In the aftermath of Winter Storm Uri, that principle became our North Star. Our work had two parallel tracks: cooperation and improvement. First, as I've mentioned previously, we committed to full transparency. We cooperated completely with investigations—state, federal, and internal—because the only way to prevent another disaster was to learn, and let others learn, from our mistakes. We opened the books, shared the data, and told the truth, even when it hurt.

Then came the harder work: looking inward. Admitting imperfection is not weakness; it's leadership maturity. We asked ourselves, *What could we have done better?* We didn't ask this as a rhetorical exercise but as a survival mandate, our goal not to assign guilt but to build resilience. We committed to being unafraid of critique, because fear of criticism is what blinds organizations to the next crisis forming on the horizon. Our mission was far larger than anyone's ego—it was to protect both the company and the state from facing that kind of failure ever again.

Leadership had stopped being theoretical. It had become visceral. Responsibility was no longer a concept but the difference between ruin and recovery, between shame and strength. I've learned that once you've led through a crisis like 9/11 or Winter Storm Uri, you never see leadership the same way again. Those two events changed me in ways that ultimately made me a better leader and taught me that responsibility isn't something you hold but something that holds you.

The Illusion of Composure

During a crisis, especially one as devastating and systemically shattering as Winter Storm Uri, the psychological toll is beyond anything leadership manuals prepare you for. You can rehearse emergency protocols, run tabletop exercises, and build resilience plans for years, but when the grid fails and chaos swallows structure, the human mind becomes the true battleground. I remember walking away for a brief moment of solitude, knowing I needed to physically and emotionally step back from the battlefield. This wasn't retreat but strategy. Clarity demands space. Sometimes, leadership means pausing amid the noise long enough to think, not react. In that fragile silence, it becomes essential to speak with your most trusted advisors, those who reflect reality back to you without distortion, grounding you when your internal compass starts spinning.

Even in those moments of internal struggle, you must project one critical quality to your team: emotional stability. Leadership during crisis is often parental in nature. You cannot afford to fall apart in front of your people any more than a parent can collapse in front of a terrified child. Your team is looking to you to determine their own reactions, whether to panic or persevere. My instinct was always to be calm, smiling even when it felt unnatural, radiating confidence even when doubt clawed at the edges of my mind, and saying with conviction that everything would be OK. It wasn't that I always believed it, but my team needed to believe it long enough to keep moving forward.

Modern leaders must also be deeply self-aware: of their own limits, their breaking points, and their humanity. There are moments in every major crisis when you have what I call a *holy shit* moment, when the weight of what's happening hits your nervous system like a physical blow. If you pretend you're invincible, you're not only exhausting yourself but also lying to your people. Authenticity matters as much as composure. Leadership isn't about suppressing emotion; it's about managing its visibility and channeling it constructively. Modeling emotional honesty while maintaining authority is the tightrope every leader must learn to walk.

When catastrophe strikes, fear spreads like wildfire. The first instinct of many employees isn't concern for the company but their own survival: *Am I going to lose my job?* During Winter Storm Uri, I saw that fear firsthand. The rulebook that had defined people's careers—the very operating system they were trained to trust—was suddenly worthless. Engineers, traders, and operators were thrust into improvisation, terrified that any wrong move might end their careers. I had to absorb that fear by making it clear that judgment would not fall on them. I said it explicitly: "This is on me. This was an executive decision." Absolving them of mistakes freed them to act. Paralysis is the enemy in crisis, and fear is its cudgel.

Taking on your team's fear doesn't erase your own. Once I had told them not to worry about their jobs, I was left with a quiet question: *Will I lose mine?* To survive the storm, keep the system alive, and still carry that uncertainty in your gut is a level of isolation few outside leadership will ever understand. You learn what it means to be the last line of defense, the emotional sinkhole for everyone else's fear. It's a loneliness that doesn't show up in any job description, but it is at the core of leadership under fire.

The Necessity of Vulnerability and Healing

One of the most profound differences between my experiences during 9/11 and Winter Storm Uri was how the concept of healing entered the equation. In 2001, mental health wasn't even part of leadership's vocabulary in the business world. The unspoken expectation was simple and absolute: Tough it out, make money, rebuild, move forward. There was pride in endurance and a quiet shame attached to struggle.

To our credit, we did endure—at least externally. The company survived. Profits eventually returned. Operations resumed. We celebrated bouncing back as evidence of our grit and resilience, but there was internal corrosion. The invisible damage went unspoken, buried beneath our collective determination to appear fine. I now recognize that my failure to acknowledge the human dimension—the exhaustion, the fear, the trauma—was a blind spot that cost us more than we realized. People came back to work, but many were hollowed out, emotionally detached, operating from muscle memory rather than renewed purpose. We achieved recovery without restoration, growth without grounding. That was my mistake, one that took years to understand.

Winter Storm Uri changed that. This time, there was an institutional recognition that we could not ignore the psychological impact. We had learned that survival alone was not the metric of success; restoration had to be part of the equation. We declared openly, "We care about the mental health of our people," and I made sure those weren't just words printed in a memo or mouthed at a town hall. I told the team I would be attending counseling sessions myself, not as a symbolic gesture or a PR moment, but as an act of leadership through participation. If I was asking others to face their pain, I had to lead by example. That single decision shifted everything. It gave permission. It made vulnerability legitimate. When your leader sits beside you, not above you, the dynamic changes from authority to shared humanity.

We brought in a licensed therapist who understood trauma-informed recovery. We created spaces—literal and emotional—where team members could share their stories without judgment or consequence. It became clear how much unspoken pain people had been carrying. One person admitted he couldn't sleep through the night anymore because he was worried he would lose his job. Even the lawyer embedded with us during the crisis—the man whose job it was to clinically document every excruciating decision—confessed that he didn't know where to start unpacking it all. He asked if he could join my counseling session. That moment was both humbling and healing. It reminded me that no title, no degree, and no amount of professional detachment inoculates you from trauma. We are all human first, leaders and colleagues second.

Embracing vulnerability, I came to understand, is not a sign of weakness but an evolved form of strength. Leadership has long been equated with stoicism, with the unflinching ability to suppress emotion for the sake of clarity and control. But the truth is, resilience and repression are not the same thing. One sustains; the other corrodes. Resilience allows you to bend and recover. Repression only guarantees eventual fracture. When leaders show up authentically—even at less than full capacity—they create psychological permission for everyone else to do the same. It signals that worth isn't tied to perfection and that honesty is a form of contribution. Sometimes the greatest leadership act is not charging into the fray but stepping back—allowing others the space to care for their families, to grieve, to rebuild the private foundations of their lives before they rejoin the collective mission.

During Winter Storm Uri, several employees were working remotely while dealing with personal crises: flooded homes, frozen pipes, children sick from the cold. I remember one employee calling in from her car, trying to get a Wi-Fi signal because her home had lost power. I told her—and others in similar situations—"Go. Fix your home. Take care of your family. Your family matters more than this company right now." Because a person whose mind is consumed with personal crisis cannot meaningfully contribute to professional recovery. By creating the space for people to stabilize their lives, we ensured that when they did return, they came back whole, grateful, and committed.

This is tempered leadership: the maturity to recognize that long-term performance depends on short-term compassion. A team that feels seen and protected and is allowed to heal becomes capable of performing miracles when the next storm inevitably arrives. Caring for the person ultimately serves the mission, a paradox that took me two decades to learn. True leadership, I discovered, is not about being the last person standing or the hero in the rubble. There's no one left for you to lead when that happens. Leaders ensure that when you're finally able to sit down, the people around you still have the strength—and the heart—to rise again. Leadership is the quiet courage to value healing as much as achievement, knowing that resilience is built not through the denial of pain but through its honest acknowledgment and collective repair.

The Alexander Comparison: What Not to Do

Throughout this book, Alexander the Great serves as a recurring mirror—sometimes reflecting the highest, purest form of decisive, strategic leadership, and at other times exposing the darker underbelly of unchecked ambition. His life serves as both myth and manual, an instruction guide for courage, vision, and relentless pursuit but also a cautionary tale about the costs of power untempered by self-awareness. His legacy remains one of history's greatest paradoxes. He stands as both the archetype of bold leadership under pressure and the embodiment of how triumph, left unexamined, becomes tyranny.

In the chapters that follow, where I explore leadership amid crisis, uncertainty, and recovery, Alexander's campaigns serve as a remarkably relevant backdrop. His military strategies—his ability to coordinate supply chains across continents, to bridge cultural differences within his ranks, and to maintain unity in the face of nearly impossible odds—offer lessons in operational brilliance and team cohesion that resonate even today. Yet when it comes to what happens after the conquest, including the emotional aftermath of victory, the loneliness of command, and the struggle to regulate one's own ego, Alexander becomes a warning rather than an inspiration. His genius on the battlefield was beyond question, but his blind spots in the aftermath were catastrophic.

Alexander never lost a major battle. From Granicus to Issus to Gaugamela, his record gleams with an unbroken string of victories that reshaped the ancient world. But within that perfection lay the very seed of his undoing. Because he never experienced true defeat, he never developed the emotional endurance that modern leaders must cultivate in the face of failure—the humility to pause, the perspective to reflect, and the adaptability to rebuild. Failure is not simply an obstacle. It refines judgment. Without failure and the resulting reflection, confidence calcifies into arrogance. Alexander's life illustrates this with painful clarity. His relentless success created the illusion that he was not merely favored by fortune but chosen by destiny, perhaps even by the gods. Over time, that belief evolved into something more dangerous: the conviction that he was infallible. When a leader confuses external success with internal virtue, when accomplishment becomes indistinguishable from identity, their fall ceases to be a matter of *if* and becomes a matter of *when*.

The absolute power Alexander held slowly corrupted and devoured him from within. Early in his campaigns, he was known for his openness. He sought counsel from philosophers, generals, and trusted companions, most notably his lifelong friend Hephaestion. He listened, debated, and occasionally changed course. But as his empire expanded, so did the echo chamber around him. The once-collaborative circle of commanders became an increasing chorus of sycophants. The distance between the leader and the led widened until the only voice left was Alexander's own.

Power without reflection breeds blindness. For Alexander, that blindness expressed itself in erratic behavior—bursts of rage, paranoia, and self-medication through drink. Later accounts depict a man who once had embodied composure and strategy gradually unraveling into impulsive outbursts and destructive emotional excesses. In modern vernacular, we would call it *burnout*—psychological unraveling under the relentless strain of unchecked responsibility and the absence of trusted counsel.

One of the clearest expressions of this unraveling came at the Hyphasis River, discussed in an earlier chapter. After years of conquest and endless marches, Alexander's exhausted army refused to continue deeper into India. These were not mutineers or cowards but men who had followed Alexander through deserts, mountains, and enemy strongholds. Their refusal to continue was more of a strike than a rebellion. The soldiers were human, and they had reached the outer limits of endurance. When they refused to go on, Alexander was stunned. The man whose charisma moved armies faced a collective wall of silence. At that moment, leadership by inspiration decayed into leadership by command, as soldiers who had once adored Alexander now resisted him. The Hyphasis episode stands as one of history's earliest recorded moments of emotional mutiny—a rebellion not of swords but of spirit. It reveals what happens when leaders fail to account for the emotional and physical exhaustion of their people, when purpose becomes pursuit for its own sake.

Alexander's greatest failure, however, did not arrive on any battlefield. It came in his final days, when he neglected to plan for what would come after him. For all his tactical brilliance, he never developed a strategy for succession. He left behind no named heir, no clear command structure, and no enduring framework to hold the vast territories he had united. Within months of his death, the empire collapsed under the weight of competing ambitions. Alexander's once-loyal generals—Ptolemy, Seleucus, Antigonus—carved his creation into fragments. He had built an empire in thirteen years, but it did not survive thirteen months. It was the ultimate irony: The conqueror of the known world was undone not by an enemy but by his own inability to delegate, to institutionalize wisdom, and to surrender control—in modern leadership terms, by the refusal to design systems resilient enough to outlast their founder. It was the quintessential unforced error.

I think of my pre-9/11 "swagger." We were making money, times were good, and there was no reason to believe they would not stay that way. I was untested by the fires of crises. I was naive. My post-Uri leadership journey required the opposite orientation. I had to learn to synthesize Alexander's strengths—his decisiveness in the face of chaos, his ability to inspire loyalty through vision, and his fearless execution under pressure—while deliberately avoiding his weaknesses of arrogance, isolation, and emotional volatility. Like him, I knew what it meant to lead through crisis, to rally a team in the face of existential threat. But unlike him, I knew I had to embrace the humility that follows survival. Victory, whether ancient or modern, can be intoxicating. It convinces leaders that momentum is permanent, that outcomes bend to willpower. Leadership after crisis requires a different kind of strength—a quieter, steadier courage. It demands reflection, patience, and the discipline to seek counsel rather than command action.

Where Alexander saw vulnerability as weakness, I came to see it as evolution. Where he demanded loyalty through hierarchy, I sought to earn it through shared accountability. Where he silenced dissent, I encouraged debate. His story reminds me that the rock star mentality—the myth that a single charismatic figure can outshine the system—is a siren song that leads even the greatest minds toward self-destruction. Empires, whether ancient kingdoms or modern organizations, do not endure because of one person's brilliance. They endure because their leaders invest in others, create mechanisms for trust, and allow power to circulate rather than accumulate.

Alexander the Great remains one of history's most illuminating figures not because he was flawless, but because his flaws are ubiquitous. His life is a case study in the psychology of power, the seductive nature of success, and the human cost of unexamined ambition. He shows us that leadership without introspection leads to isolation, and isolation without vulnerability leads to ruin. My own path after Winter Storm Uri demanded that I confront those truths personally: I needed to lead boldly, yes, but also to rest when weary, listen when uncertain, and share the burden when the weight became too heavy. That, I've learned, is how leaders transcend crisis—not by clinging to the myth of invincibility but by embracing the shared humanity that allows their teams, and their legacies, to rise again after the storms have passed.

Choosing Integrity After the Storm

The aftermath of Winter Storm Uri brought with it not only financial devastation but also unrelenting public and institutional scrutiny. The damage wasn't confined to the balance sheet; it rippled into boardrooms, newsrooms, and courtrooms. The headlines came fast, the questions faster. State regulators demanded explanations. Shareholders wanted accountability. Even industry peers were quietly watching to see whether we would be blamed or vindicated. The storm had shredded infrastructure, rattled markets, and tested the limits of human endurance, but what followed tested something even more fragile: trust. Every decision we had made during those chaotic, freezing days was being dissected by people who had the benefit of time, context, and hindsight that we never did.

This was not a simple audit of numbers or a procedural review of operations. It was a forensic examination of leadership itself, a line-by-line, moment-by-moment reconstruction of our choices under pressure. Every call, every trade, every operational pivot was scrutinized with the implicit question, *What were they thinking?* Behind that question was another, more corrosive one: *Were they acting in good faith?*

The emotional toll of existing under that microscope cannot be overstated. You find yourself reliving the worst hours of your professional life while trying to justify decisions that were made to prevent catastrophe in context. You are forced to reinhabit the very fear, exhaustion, and chaos you've spent months trying to process and put behind you.

Through all of it, my convictions were anchored in one guiding principle: radical transparency. From the very beginning, I told my team that we would cooperate fully with regulators, shareholders, auditors, and investigators and disclose everything. No half-truths, no omissions, no strategic ambiguity. I repeated the same phrase over and over, almost as a mantra: "We have nothing to hide." This wasn't a PR slogan; it was a moral stance. It set the tone for how we would respond—not as defendants but as truth-tellers. I instructed every department head, every executive, and every trader: Speak plainly, even if the truth makes us look imperfect. Let the record reflect reality, not a rehearsed version of it.

The only way to preserve credibility was to show the investigators what we had actually lived through: the triaging, the sleepless nights, the fog of decision-making under duress. I wanted them to see the crisis not as a sequence of cold transactions but as a human drama of impossible trade-offs made in real time with imperfect data, because that was the truth. We were not villains or victims but human beings doing our best in extraordinary circumstances.

There were two motivations behind this insistence on total openness. The first was deeply ethical and personal: We had acted with integrity throughout the crisis. Every call we made—however controversial in hindsight—was rooted in the intent to protect the company, the grid, and the public interest. I believed, perhaps naively at first but later with certainty, that the truth itself would vindicate us. I did not view transparency as a risk but as an affirmation of our values.

The second motivation was strategic and institutional. Radical transparency wasn't just about surviving scrutiny; it was about learning. If we wanted our organization, and indeed our industry, to grow stronger from this ordeal, we had to expose the uncomfortable parts. Concealment breeds repetition. If we buried our mistakes, the next generation of leaders would stumble over the same stones. To me, transparency was both an act of accountability and an investment in resilience. It was our way of transforming pain into institutional wisdom.

As a student of history, I know the adage, as we all do. "Those who fail to learn from history are doomed to repeat it," attributed in various forms to people from Winston Churchill to George Santayana. It is a profound truth.

I had made this decision about transparency long before the storm reached its peak, a decision rooted in the hard lessons I learned during 9/11. Back then, I had discovered how impossible it was to reconstruct decisions after the fact, once the adrenaline fades and memories blur. In the chaos of a true crisis, context is everything—and without contemporaneous documentation, context evaporates. This is why, during Winter Storm Uri, I preemptively ensured that a single trusted attorney was embedded within our operations team from the outset. His assignment was simple but essential: to document, in real time, every major action, rationale, and risk assessment as it happened. He was not there merely as legal counsel but as a silent chronicler—a witness to the chaos, capturing the anatomy of our decisions before hindsight could distort them.

That decision proved invaluable. When the investigations began, we didn't have to rely on hazy recollections or selective memory. We had a living record, a time-stamped and factual chronicle of the storm's progression and our corresponding actions. We could walk regulators through every phase of our crisis management process: when we first recognized the grid instability, how we prioritized safety, why we made specific trades or curtailments, and what information we had at each juncture. The record revealed not recklessness but reason under impossible conditions. It humanized our process while providing a shield of verifiable truth.

Reconstructing what happens in the fog of crisis is never easy. Crises are not linear; they're chaotic, looping, recursive. You make decisions, then unmake them. You pivot, adapt, and often improvise. In those moments, instinct becomes your only policy manual. All of this is happening under intense psychological stress. Having that embedded legal observer meant that when the storm had passed, we didn't have to reconstruct history through the veil of emotion; we had already preserved it as it happened. That documentation was proof of how we survived and a guide for how to respond better the next time.

In the end, the transparency we practiced satisfied oversight but became the foundation for something far more enduring: trust. Trust with regulators, who saw that we were willing to be open with our books and our intentions. Trust with shareholders, who recognized that honesty—not spin—would protect their investments. Perhaps most importantly, it built trust with our own people, who saw that our leadership wasn't about self-preservation but about collective integrity. The storm tested our infrastructure, but the aftermath tested our ethics. The fire under leadership isn't extinguished when the lights come back on. It extends into how you tell the story afterward. Leaders are measured not just by how they act in crisis but by how they account for it afterward: truthfully, fearlessly, and with the unwavering intent to leave those who follow better prepared than they ever were.

Acceptance and Moving Forward

The psychological strain on the team was unmistakable, almost palpable in the air. In the days and weeks that followed Winter Storm Uri, the mood across the organization shifted dramatically, from urgency to exhaustion. The usual noises and rhythms of our office—the hum of hallway conversations, the bursts of laughter between meetings, the quick cadence of collaboration—fell silent. The building itself seemed subdued. Lights were dimmer. Voices were softer. People lingered less at coffee stations and more at their desks, lost in thought. The silence wasn't peaceful. It was heavy, dense with fear, fatigue, and the quiet despair of those who had seen too much and slept too little. It felt as though the entire Texas team had exhaled and forgotten to start breathing again.

Everyone was spent. The people who had been so steadfast during the storm now looked hollowed out. Sleepless eyes stared blankly at screens, shoulders slumped from carrying invisible burdens. Even the most resilient showed cracks. The collective energy that once defined our team—the confident rhythm of people who knew their craft—had been replaced by something fragile and uncertain. We were united not by triumph, as had been our way as leaders and successful employees, but by trauma. The true cost of the storm—financial, reputational, and psychological—was only beginning to surface, and there was a pervasive sense that the worst damage might still be unseen. I could see it in every small hesitation, every nervous glance during meetings. People spoke in shorter sentences. Jokes fell flat. Optimism felt forced. The Texas team was functioning, but it was emotionally wounded. Limping along.

The path to real recovery always begins with validation. Before a person can heal, someone has to name the pain. They must say out loud that what you endured was real, that what you carried was heavy, and that the exhaustion you feel isn't a weakness but the natural response of a human being stretched to their limit. For me, that moment of validation came months later, when someone whose opinion I deeply respected looked directly at me and said four simple words: "It's not your fault."

I can still recall the pause that followed, the way the room seemed to soften. Up until that moment, I had been replaying the crisis on a mental loop: every decision, every trade, every sleepless night. I had carried the unspoken belief that as the leader, every failure, every loss, every hardship ultimately rested on my shoulders. That's the invisible burden of leadership—this instinct to absorb the collective pain and blame for outcomes beyond your control. Hearing someone else, especially a peer in authority, acknowledge that the catastrophe was bigger than any one person, freed me from that self-imposed sentence. It didn't erase the pain, but it allowed me to begin healing from it. The loop stopped its endless cycle in my head—oh, it still came on at times, but the whirring in the background quieted.

Leaders are trained, overtly or not, to be emotional shock absorbers. We take the impact so others don't have to. We put on calm faces, deliver reassuring words, and project control even when we're breaking inside. But every human being has a limit. The same strength that allows a leader to endure can become their prison if they never release the pressure. Silence becomes corrosive. Stoicism turns to self-destruction. What I learned through Winter Storm Uri is that validation of your wounds—especially from outside yourself—is the first step in transforming trauma into growth. It reminds you that leadership doesn't mean being superhuman; it means being honest about your humanity.

Once I heard those words—"It's not your fault"—I could finally reframe the storm not as a personal failure but as a shared experience of endurance. I began to see that leadership under crisis is not about controlling outcomes but about standing in the chaos with integrity.

You do what you can, with what you have, in the moment you're given. The rest is grace.

When I reflect on this now, I often find myself thinking of Alexander the Great—not the mythic conqueror we read about in textbooks but the young man who charged into every battle at the front of the line. In his youth, Alexander's courage was kinetic, almost theatrical. He inspired others by sheer audacity, led by demonstrating fearlessness. There is an undeniable power in that form of leadership. It rallies people when hope is scarce. Yet that same drive carries an inherent danger: It makes leaders believe they must always be the strongest person in the room, incapable of fatigue or fear. My post-Uri self came to understand a different, more mature form of courage—the courage to slow down, to reflect, to admit that not all battles are meant to be won by force.

True courage, I learned, lives not in the act of conquest but in the aftermath, in the quiet moments when you must confront your own doubts, regrets, and fatigue. The tempered leadership that emerges from failure is infinitely more valuable than the impulsive bravery that drives people into battle. Alexander's form of courage moved armies, but it also isolated him. My goal after Winter Storm Uri was to move hearts. To rebuild not just structures and systems but the confidence and trust of those who had followed me through the storm.

The crisis changed my definition of leadership forever. The old metrics of revenue, performance, and market share no longer felt sufficient. Leadership could no longer be measured by how well we maximized profit; it had to include how well we preserved people. The questions that mattered most became the profoundly human ones: *Are my people OK? Are they safe? Did we act with integrity, even when it hurt?* Success wasn't solely about expansion anymore; it was about endurance. Our mission evolved from "winning" to "stewarding"—

protecting the light during the darkest hours, ensuring that even when systems failed, our values didn't. That was what mattered most.

Healing, I've since learned, is never linear. It unfolds in waves. The first phase is operational—you fix what's broken, you restore what can be restored. But the deeper phase, the human one, is slower. It requires patience, empathy, and deliberate attention. It's the stage where real legacies are forged. If leaders want to leave behind something more meaningful than numbers or reports, they must invest in emotional literacy, both their own and that of their people. They must teach that leadership is as much about understanding fear and fatigue as it is about vision and execution.

The next generation of leaders needs more than strategic playbooks and model scenarios. They need emotional frameworks. They must be trained to think critically under stress, to interpret silence as data, to recognize when their teams are breaking even before anyone says a word. They must know how to care without rescuing and how to empathize without collapsing. In short, they must learn to lead as humans first and executives second.

And that lesson begins with us. Leaders must model that it's OK to feel pain, to admit exhaustion, to say, "I need help." That isn't weakness; it's the highest form of wisdom. When you process pain honestly, it stops being poison and becomes instruction. Scars become maps—guides for those who follow.

In *Kafka on the Shore*, novelist Haruki Murakami wrote, "And once the storm is over, you won't remember how you made it through, how you managed to survive. You won't even be sure whether the storm is really over. But one thing is certain. When you come out of the storm, you won't be the same person who walked in. That's what this storm's all about."[4]

The ultimate goal is not merely to survive the storm but to be transformed by it. To be more aware, more grounded, and more compassionate. True, resilient leaders understand that we cannot be perfect and that we don't have to stay broken when we're faced with a brutal reality. We can, must, and *do* rebuild, again and again, from the inside out. The best leaders don't just restore systems—they restore souls, beginning with their own.

---

4   Haruki Murakami, *Kafka on the Shore* (Vintage, 2006).

CROSSING NEW RIVERS

We are what we repeatedly do. Excellence, then,
is not an act, but a habit. –Aristotle

The wreckage had been cleared, both literally and figuratively. The pipes had thawed, the grid had stabilized, and the debris—emotional, operational, and financial—had finally begun to settle. We had survived Winter Storm Uri, a storm that tested our infrastructure and our very humanity. Survival brought relief, but it also brought reckoning. There's a strange quiet that follows catastrophe, the kind that amplifies every thought you tried to suppress in the chaos. In that quiet, you begin to untangle responsibility from blame.

The truth is, surviving a crisis only proves endurance, not evolution. Survival is the prerequisite for true leadership; transformation is about being called to face what follows. Once the emergency lights fade and the adrenaline drains from your veins, you face harder questions. How do you take the devastation—the sheer psychological and financial carnage—and forge it into something lasting?

That is the journey across the next river—the metaphorical Indus, if we see it through the lens of Alexander's career—the place where one chapter of conquest ends and another begins. This section of the book is dedicated to that crossing: the act of applying hard-won experience to the unknown territories ahead.

The Indus Principle

What I call the Indus principle in this book is a philosophy rooted in Alexander the Great's own moment of reckoning at the Hyphasis River, a moment historians often refer to as the edge of his empire. It was where, after years of relentless conquest, Alexander's men refused to march farther. They had reached their physical and emotional limits. Standing at the banks of the river that marked the gateway to India, Alexander confronted a profound truth: Even the greatest vision must yield to human capacity. His legendary ambition collided with mortality, fatigue, and the collective will of others. It was there, on the banks of that river, that the myth met the reality.

For modern leaders, the Indus principle represents the moment after a crisis when ambition must mature into wisdom. It's the point at which you stop asking, *How do I win?* and start asking, *What is worth winning?* If Alexander could maintain his insatiable curiosity and intellectual drive even after devastating campaigns, then modern leaders—tested by crises both physical and metaphorical—must do the same. Knowledge without application is wasted experience. We cannot allow the wisdom acquired in the fire to turn to ashes once the crisis has passed.

Wisdom over Bravado

One of the most profound internal shifts I experienced post-Uri was the transformation from bravado to wisdom. When we're young, leadership often masquerades as *motion*. Confidence is conflated with certainty, and speed with strategy. "Success" is a Google calendar so full that no one could find a spare five minutes if they tried.

I was in my early thirties during 9/11—a time defined by action, by adrenaline, by the belief that leadership meant charging in first and thinking later. That kind of courage has its place. In moments of acute crisis, boldness can save lives and companies alike. But over time, if it goes unchecked, bravado becomes blindness.

Prior to Winter Storm Uri, I had accumulated more than a decade of wins, fourteen years of consistent growth, achievement, and forward motion. The longer you ride a streak like that, the easier it is to mistake luck for skill and momentum for mastery. It becomes easy to believe you can outthink every obstacle, outwork every challenge, and outlast every storm. Success creates an illusion of control. And when the illusion shatters, as it inevitably does, the impact is Superman left powerless by Kryptonite. If Superman's identity as the Man of Steel is gone, who is he? Merely human.

For me, both 9/11 and Winter Storm Uri humbled me to my core. Each time, after the dust settled and I realized how close we had come to losing everything, I found myself overwhelmed not by pride but by gratitude: I still had a company, a job, a team, a purpose. I also felt relief and gratitude for the lives that were saved while mourning those whom we lost.

When you've been knocked from the horse, the way you ride when you get back in the saddle changes. You no longer charge into every battle. You study the terrain first. You ask questions that, in your earlier years, would have sounded like hesitation but are actually the language of wisdom. *Should we run down the hill or walk down the hill? Do we have to fight this fight at all, or can we find another way?* You begin to recognize both that some victories aren't worth the casualties and that leadership is as much about restraint as it is about action.

The older, wiser self learns to discern between battles that matter and battles that merely feed the ego. This is the fundamental difference between bravado and wisdom: Bravado acts to prove, while wisdom acts to preserve. The mature leader knows that not every hill is worth dying on, and not every fight leads to progress. There are things you simply cannot win, and accepting that truth doesn't make you weak—it makes you durable and resilient.

Redefining Success

In the aftermath of Winter Storm Uri, our team had to redefine what *success* meant. The old scorecards and traditional metrics—profit margins, performance charts, KPIs, quarterly earnings, year-over-year growth—suddenly felt sterile, almost absurdly detached from what we had just endured. Numbers, once a source of pride, were revealed as incomplete truths. They said nothing about the human cost of survival. They couldn't measure exhaustion, courage, or integrity. They couldn't quantify the look in someone's eyes when they showed up to work after losing power at home, or the quiet determination of employees who chose to serve others while their own homes were too cold to be livable.

For the first time, the questions that guided our leadership were not operational but deeply human. *Are our people safe? Are they OK? Did we act honorably in the chaos? Did we make decisions that reflect who we claim to be?* These became our moral anchors in an environment still thick with uncertainty. They grounded us when spreadsheets and projections offered no comfort and, in fact, could make you pretty queasy. We learned that leadership after catastrophe couldn't be measured by financial recovery alone; it also had to be measured by ethical recovery and how we treated those who suffered beside us. Dignity, how we stood by our values when it would have been easier to hide behind excuses or self-interest, was a measure of success in a way dollars couldn't touch.

That redefinition required a recalibration of ambition itself. We had to acknowledge that some of the goals we'd set before the storm—stretch targets, aggressive timelines, expansion plans—were no longer realistic. Clinging to them would only deepen the wounds. Leadership maturity begins with knowing when to release an expectation that no longer serves your people. The metaphor I often use is simple: Expecting a high school baseball team to beat the New York Yankees isn't ambition; it's self-destruction. It's a failure of realism disguised as drive.

We had to let go of our obsession with appearing invincible. For years, high performance had been our cultural currency. We prided ourselves on "doing the impossible." But a big enough crisis changes that equation entirely. In moments like Winter Storm Uri, the point isn't to *prove* your strength—it's to *preserve* it. Real resilience doesn't mean bouncing back to the old normal; it means constructing a wiser one.

That shift from bravado to resilience changed how we led, planned, and even thought. We began developing what I now call *resilient goals*—objectives grounded not in fantasy but in the hard soil of reality. Resilient goals acknowledge both capacity and consequence. They recognize that people have limits and that organizations, like individuals, cannot endure perpetual strain without fracture. Their development involves digging deep and asking better questions: *Can we sustain this ethically? Can we grow without eroding our values? Can we withstand the next storm without fracturing the people who hold this organization together?*

Answering those questions became the new measure of leadership maturity. Because the real test of a leader is not how high they climb in good times but how consciously they rebuild in hard ones. Anyone can chase growth when the wind is at their back, but only those with discipline and empathy can grow wisely when the world has stopped turning.

One aspect of redefining success after crisis is no longer equating achievement with acceleration. You start to see the strength in steadiness and the progress in patience. You realize that resilience is not reactive but strategic. You integrate these ideas when preparing your people, your systems, and your own mindset to weather the next storm with greater clarity and less collateral damage. It's what separates leaders who survive from those who evolve.

Over time, this redefinition became part of our shared cultural inheritance. We began teaching it, institutionalizing it, embedding it into every decision-making framework we used. Because winning at the expense of integrity, health, or trust is not victory. The question was no longer *Can we win?* but *Can we win well?* The leaders who emerged from Uri didn't merely want to recover; they wanted to endure with grace. The lesson we carried forward was that resilience is not just the capacity to recover but the courage to redefine what recovery means.

The Next River

Standing on the banks of the Indus—literally for Alexander, metaphorically for us—is the moment when a leader must confront sustainability. There, where ambition meets endurance, the question shifts from *How far can we go?* to *How long can we last?* The Indus is the line between expansion and exhaustion, between what can be conquered and what can be sustained.

For Alexander, it was a physical river marking the edge of his empire. For modern leaders, it is the invisible boundary between progress and overreach, the point where pushing harder stops being strategic and starts being self-destructive. Winter Storm Uri was my Indus. It stripped away the illusion that strength is defined by constant motion. Crossing that river demanded a new definition of power— one measured not in scale but in sustainability.

I had to evolve from conqueror to custodian, from aggressor to architect. That shift meant understanding that resilience isn't simply bouncing back but also building forward with purposeful balance. Leadership cannot be fueled indefinitely by adrenaline, ambition, or willpower. Those resources are renewable, of course, but only if you protect them. The new challenge was not to win more battles but to sustain the team, the mission, and myself for the long term.

Sustainability, in this context, means designing systems—human and organizational—that can withstand pressure without collapsing. Leaders must do so in a way that preserves capacity rather than depleting it. A sustainable culture allows people to recover, adapt, and contribute meaningfully without burning out. It values endurance over intensity and longevity over immediacy. After Winter Storm Uri, I realized that our previous definition of success—constant growth, perpetual speed, relentless performance—was not sustainable.

True leadership begins where the illusion of invincibility ends. The goal is not to win endlessly or expand indefinitely but to keep working wisely, preserving integrity, energy, and trust so the organization can thrive far beyond the moment. Leadership that is not sustainable is, by definition, temporary.

The Alexander Cautionary Tale

I've always admired Alexander the Great. His boldness, strategic brilliance, and ability to inspire loyalty shaped how I once viewed leadership. But when it comes to sustainability, one episode from his life stands as a profound cautionary tale—the Siege of Tyre. It is one of history's most striking examples of what happens when endurance crosses over into obsession and military genius erodes into personal vengeance.

In 332 BCE, Alexander set his sights on visiting Tyre, a wealthy island city, to worship and make a sacrifice at the Temple of Melqart. But when he arrived, the people denied him entry, believing that Alexander was plotting to gain easy access to the city and overthrow it. Tyre was a strategic necessity for maritime dominance of the eastern Mediterranean, and especially after being rebuffed, Alexander's personal drive for glory and retribution made ensuring his entry to Tyre an all-or-nothing endeavor. His refusal to negotiate a lesser submission suggests that ego played a role in escalating a full-on assault. To reach the city, Alexander ordered the construction of an enormous causeway—a half-mile bridge of stone and debris—to connect the mainland to the island fortress. It took seven grueling months of labor, during which countless soldiers and engineers died under relentless enemy fire. Every day, progress was measured in inches. In the end, Alexander won. The city fell, and the world marveled at his determination.

As I've mentioned earlier in this book, the conquest of Tyre is still looked to as an example of success through audacious innovation. But the victory came at a human cost. The city's resistance was a personal slight to Alexander, fueling a vengeful response where he massacred and enslaved thousands of residents. The Siege of Tyre captures the paradox of leadership with limited wisdom: brilliance in execution paired with blindness to the ability to sustain such actions over the long term. Alexander's ingenuity and perseverance were simultaneously unmatched *and* unchecked. His ability to rally others became a double-edged sword. He could inspire people to achieve the impossible, but he could also drive them into ruin, or to their deaths on a vulnerable half-built causeway, in the process of chasing it. What began as courage and innovation, for Alexander, devolved into an obsession with proving invincibility and foreshadowed how he would become more ego-driven in the future.

In his early campaigns, Alexander practiced more sustainable leadership—he built unity and shared purpose and relied on the counsel of those around him. His energy was catalytic, multiplying the capacity of everyone he led. But as his empire expanded, the model shifted. The shared energy that once sustained his campaigns became dependency more on his will alone. The ecosystem that once thrived on collaboration contracted and hardened around a single point of failure: Alexander himself. When every decision, every movement, and every ounce of morale depends on one person, the system is by definition unsustainable.

Leadership and power without self-limitation burns out its own foundation. Alexander's empire, stretched across thousands of miles, became as fragile as it was vast. His victories were dazzling but increasingly short-lived. The same leader who had once built enduring loyalty through shared vision now commanded obedience through fear and fatigue. The siege mentality—once literal, then psychological—became a permanent state.

The lesson from Tyre applies as much to modern organizations as it does to ancient armies. When leaders push too long, too hard, and more for their own egos than the organization, the machinery of excellence begins to corrode from within. People stop seeing purpose and start seeing futility. The will that once united them becomes the weight that breaks them. Sustainability, in any system, depends on equilibrium and on knowing when effort turns into depletion or persistence into pathology.

The paths of famous start-ups and successful "unicorns" are littered with the detritus of leaders and founders who never learned this lesson. Their brilliance and drive blinded them. They mistook constant motion for momentum and conflated exhaustion with excellence. They built organizations that looked impressive in the short term but were fundamentally unsustainable. When executives brag about sleeping in the office or working eighty hours a week, skepticism is justified: That sort of thing cannot go on long term. Teams working under such leaders mirror Alexander's engineers at Tyre: loyal and capable, but slowly ground down by an endless demand to perform miracles on command.

The empire became more dependent on Alexander's charisma, pace, and personal willpower in the later years of his campaigning.

When he died, the structure could not stand on its own. There were no systems designed to sustain it and no successors empowered to preserve it. The empire that spanned continents shattered into civil war, revealing the differences between achievement and endurance and between conquest and continuity.

Modern leaders must learn what Alexander never did: Sustainability is the highest form of ambition, not its opposite. Sustainable leadership is not about scaling endlessly but scaling wisely, creating systems that thrive without burning out their people or their principles. It's about designing pace as deliberately as one designs strategy, ensuring that what is built can breathe. It's about knowing when to advance and when to fortify, when to innovate and when to rest.

To lead sustainably is to measure success in careers, not quarters. It's to treat energy—human, cultural, and moral—as a finite resource that must be protected and renewed. It's to recognize that an empire, no matter how brilliantly built, is no victory if it crumbles shortly after the emperor dies.

Leadership that endures is leadership that sustains. This is the true lesson of Alexander's story and the heart of the Indus principle. The challenge is not to keep conquering faster than can be sustained but to build something that can stand when the conquering stops.

Building a Resilient Future: Teaching Others How to Think

The highest form of leadership acquired after a crisis like Winter Storm Uri doesn't lie in telling your team *what* to think but in teaching them *how* to think. This distinction may seem subtle, but in moments of chaos, it determines the difference between paralysis and performance.

Teaching people how to think requires foresight. It is a discipline that must be practiced *before* the storm hits; it cannot be improvised in the middle of one.

When a true crisis strikes, time is a luxury you don't have. There's no room for philosophical deliberation, no space to weigh every variable. Decisions must be made in seconds, often based on fragmentary data, and are driven by instinct refined through experience and preparation. If a leader has not cultivated independent thinkers beforehand—that is, if the team has never been trained to question, analyze, and decide under pressure—then when disaster comes, they will simply look upward, waiting for orders that arrive too late. Fear fills the vacuum left by untrained thinking. Indecision spreads faster than any operational failure.

Teaching people how to think begins with a simple but transformative baseline: Everyone processes problems differently, and those differences are a strength, not a threat. Strong leadership harnesses that diversity of perspective, cultivating collective intelligence rather than enforcing uniform thought. In practice, this requires patience, humility, and the willingness to challenge assumptions—especially your own. It demands that leaders create a culture where questioning is not rebellion but responsibility.

This philosophy also redefines what preparation looks like. Before Winter Storm Uri, our preparation was quantitative, not imaginative. We believed we were ready because our models accounted for price swings of two or three standard deviations. But as the storm revealed, we had been preparing for "expected extremes," not actual anomalies. The event we faced was a move of four or five standard deviations. Statistically speaking, it was "something that should never happen." But it did. The lesson was unmistakable: The limits of imagination can become the boundaries of survival. Preparing your team to think means pushing them beyond the comfort zone of probability into the realm of possibility. It's not about predicting the unpredictable; instead, it's about building a mindset resilient enough to adapt when the unimaginable becomes reality.

After the dust settled, we made a commitment not only to capture the lessons learned but to institutionalize them to ensure they would outlast individual memories and personnel changes. We began to organize our recovery and redesign around three key pillars—process, technology, and training—the structural triad of sustainable leadership intelligence.

PROCESS: PROTECTING INSTITUTIONAL MEMORY

Creative people often resist process, the discipline of capturing institutional knowledge. They equate it with bureaucracy, rigidity, and the stifling of innovation. But in a crisis, process is not the enemy of creativity—it is its anchor. Process handles the repetitive, noncreative aspects of work so that human ingenuity can be focused where it matters most. It is not about "setting and forgetting." You want to build a system durable enough to endure chaos while flexible enough to evolve. In our post-Uri world, process became the scaffolding that held the organization together when emotions and conditions were volatile.

The most immediate example of this for us was communication. During the storm, internal communication was disorganized. Some critical information didn't flow fast enough or reach the right people at the right time in departments not affiliated with operations. In the aftermath, redesigning that process became our first act of transformation. We rebuilt our communication architecture from the ground up—clarifying decision trees, codifying handoffs, and creating redundancies so that no single person or point of failure could paralyze the system. As this reimagining demonstrates, process is not about control but clarity, about creating structures that support the freedom to act during a crisis and getting the right information to the right people throughout the organization, not just within the operating teams.

TECHNOLOGY: SCALING HUMAN INTELLIGENCE

Technology is the great amplifier of process. It captures what humans should not have to remember and executes what they should not have to repeat. Investing in technology is not about replacing people—it's about preserving human energy for complex creative and moral problems that machines cannot solve.

The sustainability of any organization depends on how well it automates what can be automated while simultaneously elevating human thought where it matters most. After Uri, we began to see technology differently: not as a tool of convenience, but as a structural necessity for resilience. Automation allows organizations to encode their learning, to embed their intelligence into systems that do not fatigue or forget. Our goal was to let technology handle the cognitive muscle memory of the business—data integration, repetitive analysis, monitoring—so that our people could focus on synthesis, strategy, and leadership, particularly under stress.

In moments of crisis, when bandwidth narrows and time compresses, the best technology doesn't just increase speed; it can sustain clarity. In that sense, technology has become our silent partner in sustainability, a mechanism for preserving focus and extending human capacity without depleting it.

TRAINING AND MENTORING: SUSTAINING THE HUMAN CORE

If process and technology preserve knowledge, training and mentoring preserve humanity as the bridge between systems and souls. Leadership training is not just about technical proficiency but about emotional literacy. We realized that if we wanted to build an organization capable of withstanding crisis, we had to prepare people not only for operational complexity but for psychological endurance.

Teaching others how to think requires modeling how to feel in moments of chaos. It means demonstrating composure under pressure, empathy in decision-making, and moral clarity when the path ahead is uncertain. Training became less about memorizing procedures and more about internalizing principles—how to make ethical decisions when every option carries pain, how to steady yourself when others are unraveling, how to find purpose amid loss.

The commercial team began mentoring young leaders differently. Instead of handing them checklists, we gave them questions: *What are you solving for? Who are you serving? What assumptions might you be missing?* We taught them that leadership is less about knowing the right answers and more about asking the right questions, especially when the data is incomplete and the stakes are high. We talked openly about moral fatigue, about the loneliness of command, and about the courage required to remain compassionate when logic demands detachment.

At its highest level, leadership training becomes an act of care, an active investment in people's psychological sustainability. When crisis arrives, what carries an organization through is not just knowledge or process or even technology but the steadiness of human character.

Teaching people how to think is the ultimate form of leadership sustainability. It ensures that when the inevitable happens, your organization doesn't collapse into dependency but rises into autonomy. The goal is to create not followers but thinkers. To build not an empire of compliance but a culture of cognition.

Leaders who invest in that kind of preparation build something truly enduring: a team that can think clearly under pressure, act ethically amid ambiguity, and adapt instinctively when the future refuses to behave as planned. That is the best possible legacy of crisis leadership—not perfection but preparedness; not survival but sustainable wisdom.

The Role of the Trusted Lieutenant

You cannot be successful during the crisis or navigate the aftermath alone. The only way to avoid the isolation of command is having trusted people who hold you accountable. It is vital.

My right-hand man, Aden, was an invaluable part of my leadership team, especially in the aftermath of Winter Storm Uri. Another of my lieutenants, the unflappable Claudia, was equally irreplaceable. Each fulfilled different roles, but together, they were what allowed me the space and time to step back from the battlefield to think clearly.

Aden served as a powerful cognitive foil to my own thinking. He was never afraid to come up with ideas, no matter how risky or unconventional the situation. He helped me think, bringing raw intellectual energy to the most complex problems. He was also incredibly calm, easily able to separate himself from the unfolding chaos. He was an intense and constant thinker. Even in the middle of the fight, he could quickly generate ideas, and some of those ideas were truly exceptional.

Claudia was unflappable—a rock and a constantly calming presence. She possessed immense endurance. I entrusted her with some of the difficulties and hard stuff, knowing she would take tough assignments and relieve some of the command burden. Her particular genius lay in combining a gentle approach with a core of resilient steel. On the one hand, she was sweet and traditional, but she used that politeness to dominate. We nicknamed her "the Velvet Hammer." Claudia was a diplomat and excelled at maintaining relationships, covering a known weak spot of mine, and she was an excellent organizer, intuitively and efficiently putting things in the right order. Today, Claudia continues to apply these strengths as a senior vice president, running all of Vistra's renewables development and data centers.

After a crisis, leaders need to rely on people who can offer them two things. Some must be stronger than you are in certain areas, like Claudia. Others, like Aden, must always be centered and disconnected from immediate events. These core roles are essential to ensuring that you, the leader, can step off the battlefield, take a walk, and get clarity to avoid breaking the team.

What I learned from crossing the various rivers of crisis that have been part of my career is that ultimate success isn't about profit, status, or bravado but about establishing an authentic, resilient structure that can weather any future catastrophe. This includes not only the psychological strength of the leader but the competence and reliability of their lieutenants and the intellectual capability of a team that has been taught how to think, not merely to do.

THE ALEXANDER LEGACY

No man is an island entire of itself; every man is a piece
of the continent, a part of the main. —John Donne

The journey of leadership, especially after confronting events as cataclysmic as 9/11 and Winter Storm Uri, culminates not in the fact of survival, but in the establishment of legacy. Part III of this book, The Indus Principle: Into New Territories, has charted the transformation that follows devastation, that integration of hard-won wisdom. But the ultimate responsibility goes even further: These costly lessons, so painfully learned, must survive the leader if they are to create a lasting impact that extends beyond any single career journey.

I wrote this book because I've seen too many leaders feel profoundly unprepared when a true crisis strikes. I have been that leader. Modern leadership training often focuses on success to the exclusion of everything else, ignoring the preparation needed for failure and all that follows in its footsteps. My goal is to clearly, directly show leaders some strategic tools and emotional resources that make it more possible to handle high-pressure situations with confidence and integrity. The ultimate measure of whether I have achieved my goal of helping others learn and develop these tools and methods lies in the strength and resilience of the systems and the people I leave behind. I am thrilled to report that in my own career, those I have left behind are doing amazingly! But this doesn't happen by itself. A legacy must be built.

The Alexander Paradox: The Failure of Succession

When examining Alexander the Great's impact, we see a crucial paradox: immense, immediate victory coupled with catastrophic, long-term institutional failure. Alexander's ability to inspire loyalty was legendary: His troops followed him for ten brutal years, enduring campaigns that became increasingly difficult. His success depended on fostering mutual growth and shared victories. His companions became capable rulers themselves, embodying the successful transfer of command abilities.

However, Alexander's unbroken streak of victories meant he never truly dealt with professional failure or the crisis of confidence that accompanies loss. This success eventually bred arrogance. He became increasingly autocratic and consulted the companions who had been key to his early campaigns less and less. But his final, devastating mistake—the failure to secure his legacy—is also the most pointed lesson he provides for modern leaders.

Alexander died suddenly one night in Babylon, at just thirty-two years old. He left no clear successor, no plans for a transition. His inner circle, the Diadochi, gathered to form a plan. Tragically, their plan quickly disintegrated into a protracted and violent civil war that shattered Alexander's empire.

Even if you haven't read the history, you've seen this story play out on TV. This is the *succession* mentality, where a leader believes they are infallible and fails to prepare for their own inevitable absence. It is just as dangerous as it seems. A mature leader recognizes that preparing the organization for transition is not a sign of weakness but the highest duty of command. Alexander's failure serves as a vital blueprint for what not to do. Repeated success does not excuse the failure to prepare the next generation.

Investing in Enduring Leadership

A leader's true legacy is built upon the caliber of the leaders they develop. Alexander's initial success in training formidable companions—such as Ptolemy, who went on to rule in Egypt—demonstrates the power of investing in people. They learned how to be "real leaders" from him.

I mirrored this philosophy by intentionally investing in my core team, some for over two decades. The goal was never to hoard control but to foster people who could form solutions, rather than staring at me paralyzed by fear when crisis struck.

When developing future leaders, I look for a combination of four core traits:

1. **Competence:** They must demonstrate not mere proficiency but excellence in their role, consistently delivering

results that go beyond the baseline expectations. True competence involves mastery of their craft, continuous learning, and the ability to adapt when circumstances change. It's not enough to meet the minimum standard. They must strive to set new ones, raising the performance bar for themselves and others.

2. **Ambition:** Ambition sometimes gets a bad reputation. But it is not destructive when guided with purpose and discipline to catalyze growth. Ambition fuels innovation, propels forward motion, and inspires others to dream bigger. The key is how it is directed: Ambition should be channeled toward achieving collective goals, not personal glory. Those who possess healthy ambition see challenges as opportunities and are unwilling to settle for mediocrity.

3. **Humility and integrity:** These two qualities form the moral backbone of lasting leadership. Humility means acknowledging that no one person has all the answers. Embracing it means embracing the practice of knowing (or at least finding out) what you don't know. Humility invites curiosity, learning, and collaboration. Integrity, on the other hand, ensures that actions align with words and values, even when there is a cost. Under pressure or in the face of lucrative shortcuts, integrity demands doing the right thing. Together, humility and integrity foster trust, loyalty, and moral authority.

4. **Shared vision:** Great leaders understand that success is not a solo pursuit—it's a collective achievement. They recognize that winning is the standard expectation, not a rare event, and that true victory is built on unity. A shared

vision means every team member knows the mission, feels ownership of it, and understands their role in bringing it to life. When this alignment exists, teams operate with purpose, resilience, and pride in shared outcomes.

The transfer of leadership ability must be coupled with the transfer of institutional knowledge. It is particularly important that painful and costly lessons become practical, repeatable protocols that outlast any single leader. Leadership without codified wisdom is fragile, only one person deep. An organization's leadership becomes stronger when the hard-earned lessons of a crisis are systematically captured, analyzed, and embedded into how the organization thinks and acts. Alexander, through his long campaigns, did precisely this. He didn't just win battles; he created enduring military frameworks—supply logistics, siege strategies, and battlefield formations such as the phalanx I discussed earlier—that influenced warfare for centuries. His genius was not only tactical but institutional: He turned experience into doctrine.

Similarly, post-Uri, our mission evolved from mere survival into creating permanence. The chaos we endured had to become instruction we could transfer—a better and more diverse operational playbook built from blood, sweat, and late-night crisis calls. During the height of the storm, we were writing the playbook as we went, improvising daily under impossible conditions. Every decision carried massive stakes, every hour brought new information, and every misstep was paid for dearly. The subsequent investigations and board reviews and the staggering financial loss demanded something transformative. We could no longer rely on heroic effort; we needed disciplined systems. Radical change was not optional—it was the only responsible path forward.

Chaos around energy infrastructure is still on the rise. Demand for electricity is increasing across the country because of the electrification of home heating and transportation, the onshoring of industry, and the rapid increase in data centers. Investment in infrastructure has not kept pace, except in energy sources such as solar and wind power, which cannot instantaneously respond to power demand in real time. Archaic regulatory structures limit the incentive for companies to invest in necessary responsive and flexible energy technologies, such as natural gas and nuclear generation. The climate is increasingly producing more storms, heat waves, and cold snaps that challenge the integrity of the electric grid. Reliable and affordable electricity is the foundation of every industry on earth and is essential for the prosperity of our nation. As such, the lessons we learned from Winter Storm Uri, painful as they were, cannot remain confined to one company's experience. They must become part of how the entire energy sector—and every industry that depends on it—prepares, responds, and endures. When the grid fails, hospitals go dark, supply chains freeze, and communities suffer. The stakes demand that we move beyond reactive heroics toward proactive resilience. The next crisis isn't a question of *if*, but *when*. Will you face it as Alexander did at Tyre—with brilliant improvisation but at an unsustainable cost— or will you build systems designed to withstand the chaos before it arrives? The distinction begins with transforming crisis situations into institutional knowledge.

Institutionalizing Hard-Won Wisdom

As we saw in the previous chapter, our recovery post-Uri was guided by a focus on process, technology, and training—the structural triad of sustainable leadership intelligence. As we moved toward translating what we'd done during Winter Storm Uri into systems and protocols that could be disseminated and put into practice, we focused on fixing key breakdowns, primarily through three lenses:

1. **Process and communication:** The very first things we redesigned post-Uri were communication protocols. We realized that the escalation process was not fit to deal with the demands of disaster. We also addressed fundamental processes, such as the mandated asset status report provided daily, by ten o'clock in the morning, to the power grid operator (ERCOT). During the storm, that mandated process broke down. Fixing this required integrating the knowledge of how to protect foundational procedures.

2. **Rethinking risk and preparation:** The storm proved that standard risk models, which analyzed variations up to two or three standard deviations, were dangerously insufficient. We shifted our preparation model to examine events previously dismissed as "impossible," at four or five standard deviations. This meant tangible changes in process and practice, such as increasing fuel oil storage from two days to seven days, pre-building wind shields for certain assets, and adding more natural gas storage to the supply mix.

3. **Financial safety mechanisms:** Recognizing that the $9,000 price cap in Texas created a "winner takes all" or "casino" environment when energy prices skyrocketed, we pushed for market design changes. The industry responded by lowering the cap from $9,000 to $5,000. Crucially, we were also able to institutionalize a market circuit breaker, designed to prevent total financial carnage. This breaker

lowers the cap after twelve hours of extreme pricing, protecting cities and companies from bankruptcy.

By focusing on these changes, we ensured that the institutional memory of the crisis, reinforced by meticulous documentation (thanks to the embedded lawyer's chronicling of events), would be codified in ways that will compel future leaders to recognize a broader scope of necessary preparation.

The Challenge of Organizational Risk Aversion

After a major crisis, the temptation to become organizationally risk averse is strong. In confronting catastrophic losses and the intense investigation that follows, the immediate, paralyzing response is to retreat to the safest possible position. Tempting as it feels, though, risk aversion is actually an insidious threat.

When an organization allows itself to become paralyzed by fear, innovation dies, and the organization cannot function effectively. My counsel to emerging leaders facing this postcrisis reflex is that you cannot avoid risk by refusing to move, any more than you can simply erase fear with swagger or impatience. You must acknowledge the new reality and operate within the new constraints, understanding that success may be redefined.

Financial success is no longer just measured by the highest profit but by the answers to questions like, *What risks are we taking on with this strategy, and how bad can it get? Do we have the proper processes or insurance to handle the risks?* You must be pragmatic, recognizing that certain challenges (such as facing an overwhelming physical foe) are unwinnable. The goal becomes surviving the maelstrom while conserving resources until the environment stabilizes. Once it has, it takes patience and strategic communication to reintroduce risk. We spent years post-Uri slowly working toward the relaxation of constraints. A leader must advocate for calculated risk, proving that established systems and processes are resilient enough to handle a higher degree of uncertainty.

The process of writing this book is an extension of this practice and part of my legacy mission. Historical writings often focus solely on either dominant power or total failure, entirely neglecting the profound crisis of confidence that accompanies loss. My experiences during 9/11 taught me that the emotional toll must be addressed, and I applied that learning after Winter Storm Uri by making mental healing part of the process going forward. Having transitioned from the C-suite, my focus is now on sharing that hard-won experience, ensuring that the monumental cost of crises like Winter Storm Uri results in lasting resilience for the next generation.

This book, structured around the four phases of preparation, confrontation, aftermath, and moving forward, provides a road map for navigating the inevitable. The Alexander legacy, therefore, is defined not by any one person's career achievements but by the strength and integrity of the people and systems that carry these lessons forward.

Failure and hardship *will* come, and you must prepare for the inevitable. Operating in crisis will eventually be a reality, and so leaders must teach their teams *how* to think rather than simply *what* to think, while fostering a caring culture of empathy and respect. When everyone is prepared with core principles and a framework of disciplined thought, they will become part of the solution rather than paralyzed by fear. A team that feels cared for, understood, supported, and respected will fight not just for the company but for each other when the crisis inevitably comes—that's what you want to define your own path forward.

Our careers as leaders are rarely an elevator we ride alone to the executive suite. More often, they're a rope ladder with a few rungs missing, and we need others holding it steady as we climb. When we face a disruption during our ascent, what matters is how we respond to and learn from that obstacle and how we prepare our team for the next missing rung up ahead.

This is the Alexander legacy worth claiming: a culture of resilience that endures long after you're gone, built by leaders who prepare others to conquer the chaos they themselves may never face.

When the next crisis arrives, may it find you and your team already prepared to face it together.

CONNECT WITH STEVE

Thank you for reading *Conquering Chaos: Alexander the Great's Wisdom for Leading in Disruptive Times.* I hope this book helps you navigate your leadership journey. Feel free to connect with me at any point along the way:

Website: stevemuscato.com

LinkedIn: linkedin.com/in/steve-muscato-3956b922

For professional and media inquiries, speaking engagements, and questions about the book, you can reach me directly at smuscato@ yahoo.com.

ABOUT THE AUTHOR

Steve Muscato is a seasoned executive and crisis leadership expert whose career has been defined by navigating organizations through disruption. Over several decades in the utility industry, he has led large-scale operations during some of the most challenging events of our time, including the aftermath of 9/11, periods of economic volatility, and devastating natural disasters such as Winter Storm Uri.

His leadership philosophy is built on the belief that clarity, courage, and character are the foundation of effective decision-making. In *Conquering Chaos: Alexander the Great's Wisdom for Leading in Disruptive Times*, Muscato bridges ancient military strategy with modern business realities, revealing how lessons from history's most celebrated and controversial commander can guide leaders in today's unpredictable world. He explores both Alexander's triumphs and his failures, offering readers a balanced and practical perspective on what it truly takes to lead under pressure.

Muscato's approach combines deep operational expertise with a commitment to building resilient, united teams. He has earned a reputation for staying focused in high-stakes situations, fostering trust among colleagues, and turning moments of crisis into opportunities for growth and innovation. His work emphasizes not only how to seize opportunities but also how to recognize and avoid the missteps that can erode even the strongest leadership.

Based in Dallas, Texas, Muscato continues to mentor emerging leaders and advise organizations seeking to strengthen their ability to thrive in the face of disruption. His insights, shaped by both the victories and setbacks of his career, reflect a steadfast dedication to helping others lead boldly, wisely, and with integrity—no matter the challenge.